ISSUES OF FREEDOM

Paradoxes and Promises

WORLD PERSPECTIVES

Volumes already published

WORLD PERSPECTIVES · *Volume Twenty-three*

Planned and Edited by RUTH NANDA ANSHEN

ISSUES OF FREEDOM
Paradoxes and Promises

BY HERBERT J. MULLER

New York
HARPER & BROTHERS PUBLISHERS

Contents

PART THREE.　　RELATED IDEALS

World Perspectives

What This Series Means

WORLD PERSPECTIVES is the expression of a new vision of reality. It is a program to mark the spiritual and intellectual revolution through which humanity is passing. It aims to provide an authoritative perspective on the fundamental questions of our modern age, taking into account the changing cultural, scientific, religious, social, political, economic, and artistic influences upon man's total experience. It hopes to define through its universal principle and its individual volumes man's greater orientation in the world and the unprecedented development in men's feeling for nature and for each other.

Through the creative effort of the most responsible world leaders in thought, who have a paternity in the new consciousness and in the enlarged conceptual framework of reference of our epoch, this Series attempts to evoke not a rebirth of good will but vigorous ideas capable of overcoming misconceptions and confusing traditions and of restoring man's faith in his spiritual and moral worth and in his place in the cosmic scheme.

World Perspectives has been conceived out of a concern for the overwhelming accretion of facts which natural science has produced but upon which this science has failed, by virtue of the present limitations of its method, to bestow any adequate meaning. It is the thesis of this Series that man has lost him-

self as the living center in a world created by himself. He has
been fragmented into different categories which are the subject matter of various scientific approaches to reality with the
result that he has become a heterogeneous mass of isolated
pieces of reality, of spheres of objects. And the subjectivity
left to him has been either driven into the cognitively irrele-
vant, remote corner of the emotions or his self has been for-
malized into the logical subject of scientific analysis, leaving
him impotent to grasp the inner synthesis and organic unity
of life.

There are, however, manifestations of a slow, if reluctant,
awakening, and man as the experiencing, responsible and
deciding self, endowed by nature with freedom and will, yet
beset with confusion and isolated from the dynamic stream
of living reality, begins to recognize the ominous implications
of the loss of his center and to see that the different realms of
scientific approaches to life, to man in relation to himself and
his world, have been falsified. He is increasingly aware that his
predicament consists in his inhuman situation of being treated
and of treating himself as an object among objects, and as a
consequence his image of the unity, order and beauty of the
universe has collapsed. It is this new consciousness which
World Perspectives endeavors to define, and thus to present a
critically examined doctrine of man which may become a
healing and preserving force capable of counteracting the pro-
cedural obsessions that afflict the modern mind in our apoc-
alyptic era.

The conceptual framework of man's thinking in the West

and in the East, our authors believe, has become inadequate for understanding our world. The models and symbols that have served in the past no longer suffice; the old metaphors have lost their relevance and mankind has been emptied of its spiritual orientation and moral certitude. Our chief anxiety issues not from new experiences but from the fact that space and time, that implicit framework of all experience, have changed. Both actual life and theoretical thinking have outrun our powers of imagination. And yet our imagination is deeply influenced by those scientific notions which our reason is unable to fathom. The theoretical constructions on which the marvels of our world age are erected transcend the very language we speak, for finally they can be expressed only in mathematical symbols.

As space and time have changed their appearance and shattered our most elementary foothold in the physical world, and as language itself has undergone a mutation, we have been thrown into a state of anarchy and suspicion, conscious that science which has fathered these changes is itself threatened unless it too can be attuned to the wider and deeper range of human thought and human experience. For it appears that unless great spiritual resources are present men tend to lie prostrate, to droop as mere victims of conditions and circumstances.

World Perspectives is born out of this consciousness of man's spiritual poverty and conceptual failure. For now the question of the human meaning of man's knowledge can no longer be repressed. The qualitative uniqueness of every life process and especially the uniqueness of that process which is called human is the subject of scrutiny of this Series. It attempts to point to a dialectic of polarity in which unity and diversity are accepted as simultaneous and necessary aspects of the same essence. It is a revolt against that philosophy which neglected the existing man and turned exclusively to the structure of the world. It is an effort to show that not causality alone but relationship as well constitute the living reality capable of creating a meaningful doctrine of man. It warns of the tragic implications of the atomization of our knowledge of man and nature which though a matter of expediency is at the same time a cause for distortion. And finally, this Series is a co-operative endeavor to contribute to the construction of the new, yet ancient, morality of the new world age in the new world community by analyzing and re-defining not only the traditional and obvious ethical aspects of life but the nature of life itself including the nature of man's relationship to the universe, to himself and all mankind. Only through such reflections may those basic concepts emerge which will permit the human spirit to ride disaster and wring victory out of the extremity of defeat, vindicating human freedom and the power of human personality. For finally seminal concepts must replace rampant ideologies.

World Perspectives presents powerful thinkers, unafraid and unimpeded, fiercely and unremittingly dedicated to the universal, unitive yet paradoxical meaning of life which may emerge out of the disciplined vision of reality. The authors of this Series endeavor to be the architects of the edifice constituting this new reality through poignant concepts, basic, powerful, novel, in order that the human mind may encompass and control what the human spirit may envisage and what human hands may touch. Implicit in this Series is the commitment to new ideas which come only through the quiet dissolving of prejudices, through the influence of new conditions that give birth to new prepossessions, through a certain necessary oblivion in the handling of tradition from one generation to another and through a process of elision by which mankind can surrender to novel and enlarged points of view without at first knowing it.

The authors of *World Perspectives* hope to articulate the deep changes in men's minds that cannot be reached by logical argument, for it is a mysterious virtue in the nature of man that he is capable of working for purposes greater than those of which he may be conscious and greater than any act of volition he may make, however mighty; as though there were an invisible creative force at work in the universe, subtle and inexplicable, in the midst of confusion.

In this way, it is submitted, *World Perspectives* attempts to show that man is that unique organism in terms of matter and energy, space and time, which is urged to conscious purpose through reason, his distinguishing principle. In this way the parochial society of the past may be ultimately transformed into the universal society of the future. In this way man may be unlocked from systems of thought which imprison and destroy. And this may be achieved only if the human heart and the human mind remember that principle of life, that law of the universe, that dynamic process and structure affording man a rocklike foundation while nourishing the maximum elasticity of his intellect. And this principle, this law, remains now as ever before: Hold to the truth, to the unity of man and the unity of knowledge, to the unmediated wholeness of feeling and thought, the unity of the knower and the known, of the outer and inner, of subject and object, particle and wave, form and matter, self and not-self. As to the fragmented remainder, let us be totally uncommitted while at the same time we explore, enrich and advance the unfolding of the life process which relentlessly presses forward to actualize new forms.

New York, 1960

RUTH NANDA ANSHEN

Foreword

ALTHOUGH this work amounts to a philosophical essay, it was conceived as an introduction to a history of freedom. For this purpose I found it necessary to consider freedom in relation to culture as a whole, not merely to the state. I have likewise viewed it in a considerably longer, wider perspective than thinkers were able to before this century, in which there has been a vast deal of research in history, sociology, and anthropology. In such a perspective the subject of freedom grows more complex, and does not readily permit the logical rigor and precision to which many philosophers aspire; but I must hope that it is also illumined.

My main concern has been the basic, not the immediate issues of freedom, and my main purpose an objective analysis, not a prescription or a call to arms. Inevitably, however, I have written with the immediate issues in mind. I continually refer to them, in part for the sake of concrete illustration, but also for their own sake. And I make no pretense of utter objectivity, given a subject in which we all have deep commitments. My analysis has been influenced by preconceptions, my conclusions come down to a credo. I should maintain only that I have endeavored to lay on the table, face up, all the premises of my commitments, and that my preconceptions are not mere prejudices, unconscious or unreasoned.

Part One

The Premises of Inquiry

I.

The Meanings of Freedom

TO THE ordinary man, freedom means the feeling of being able to do as he likes, act at his own sweet pleasure. We all know and like this feeling; it always enters consciousness as "Free, hurrah!" But we also know that the good feeling never lasts. Presently, restless or discontent, we realize the truism that man never is free to do just what he pleases or only what he pleases. Then we may ask what freedom "really" means— only to get really confused. As a hurrah word, it has meant different things to different men, the more because of its liaisons with other good feelings. Mortimer Adler and a team of scholars spent several years analyzing the meanings it has had for Western thinkers, and the ordinary man might be dismayed by the report of their findings in *The Idea of Freedom,* a digest that takes up more than six hundred pages. Here it appears that philosophers have usually meant by freedom the very opposite of our sweet pleasure. "True freedom," most of them have agreed, consists in doing one's duty, being virtuous and wise, being one's "true self." They thereby confirm the popular idea that freedom is a good thing, but they do not clear up the confusion. They have never agreed on what duty and wisdom consist in or on how to recognize one's true self, tell whether it is the inner voice that cries no or the voice that cries yes. They too are talking about different things.

Common sense may now rebel, declaring that these are only verbal complications—we all know what freedom really is even if we can't put it into words. But then let us ask a natural, sensible question. America has been known all over the world as a free country, though recently some people have had doubts; and are Americans today more free or less free than they were a generation ago, before the New Deal? Or than their ancestors were a century ago on the frontier, in their rude cabins? Or than the ancient Athenians were, in a society without time clocks and stop signals? The most sensible answer might seem to be another question: Who can say?

Now, I do not assume that the confusion can be dispelled by logical or semantic rigor. We cannot give an utterly precise meaning to so broad and rich a concept as freedom, at least without arbitrarily excluding a great deal of its vital historical meaning. Neither can we hope to sterilize it, stop it from touching off hurrahs. Yet we must be able to give meaningful answers to such pertinent questions about the state of freedom if we are going to talk about the subject at all. Short of exactitude, we can aim at a relatively neutral, objective, operational definition: one that refers to roughly observable conditions, permits roughly verifiable statements about them, and so makes theoretically possible a rough agreement. In giving us pause, the questions also give us cues. They make plain that *freedom* means concretely *freedoms,* of various kinds. We cannot make out any such thing as "true" freedom in the abstract, but we can distinguish some common garden varieties, can specify in what respects some men are more or less free than others.

As the only true meanings of a word, strictly speaking, are dictionary meanings, we might at least begin by accepting common usage, based on common experience. It is remarkable, indeed, how much confusion we can avoid by clinging to the simple idea that freedom means first of all being *free* in the ordinary sense—unconfined, unfettered, unconstrained—and not necessarily dutiful, virtuous, or wise. We can never positively demonstrate that Americans are better or worse men than they used to be, but we can point to positive ways in which they are more or less confined and constrained. Then we might hope to discuss more profitably the further question of the uses and abuses of freedom, its relation to other goods.

In formal terms, *freedom* in this work will mean "the condition of being able to choose and to carry out purposes." This definition has three immediate implications: (1) the primary dictionary meaning—the absence of external constraints; (2) practicable purposes, or an actual ability with available means; and (3) a power of conscious choice, between significant, known alternatives. It accordingly involves the common ideas of freedom *from,* freedom *to,* and freedom *of,* but it leaves open the question of freedom *for* what. In simple words, a man is free in so far as he can do something or choose not to do it, can make up his own mind, can say yes or no to any given question or command, can decide for himself the matter of duty or *for* what. He is not free in so far as he is prohibited from following his inclinations or is obliged to do something against his own volition, whether by direct coercion or by fear of consequences, even though it might be better for him than his heart's desire. Granted that such statements may ring bells, they are none the less meaningful and refer objectively to a recognizable condition—a condition that feels good but may not produce further good, may lead to folly, sin, or unhappiness.

All these statements must of course be qualified. Man is always constrained by physical necessities, subject to natural law, and as he lives with his fellows he must always submit to further social constraints. Freedom is restricted only when the constraints appear to be arbitrary—unaccustomed, unnecessary, unreasonable, or unjust. The primary historical source of such restriction has been political power, the subjection of most men to the will of one or a few. Since these subjects have generally accepted as natural what seems to us arbitrary rule, we cannot readily set up a universal criterion for deciding what constraints are unreasonable or unjust. But we can begin by determining the actual constraints, by whom and on whom. We can state it as a fact that freedom is broadened in so far as arbitrary power is limited, rule is constrained by the recognition of rights, and rights are extended to all members of a society, guaranteed by law.[1] In this respect

[1] In the form of civil liberties, such rights have led some thinkers to make fine distinctions between *freedom* and *liberty,* but in common usage the terms are virtually interchangeable. The French have got along with

Americans today are certainly freer than the overwhelming majority of men ever were in the past, or than Germans were under Hitler. In recent years they have as certainly been subjected to unaccustomed constraints by security regulations and peacetime draft; though most of them have accepted these as reasonable.

The absence of external constraints has little meaning, however, until it is coupled with the positive idea of "actual ability with available means." A child dropped in the middle of a desert is freed from constraints—he no longer has to go to school, eat spinach, do chores; but he is free only to starve. As nominal was the freedom of many children who once had only a choice of factories in which to work twelve hours a day, or of the many poor who were "just as free as the rich to sleep under bridges." Effective freedom requires opportunities as well as rights. From this point of view, the major historical barrier has been not merely political oppression but poverty and ignorance. All other things equal, a man with money is freer than a man without it, an educated man freer than an illiterate. In this respect too Americans have plainly been much freer in their land of opportunity than were the masses of the past, including ordinary Athenians, and today are on the whole better off than their ancestors. They have been made so by free public education, more recently by social security and unemployment relief—by measures that have cre-

---

only one word, *liberté*. While making no real distinction, I have preferred *freedom* because it has an adjective to go with it, as *liberty* does not. *Liberal* has a specialized meaning, and may further confuse the issues because to many Americans it is a bad word.

ated new problems, involving threats to freedom, but that have nevertheless given most Americans more opportunity, more power to carry out their purposes.

Most important—and most troublesome—is the intimately related power of conscious choice, through intelligence and knowledge. Other animals are able to carry out their instinctive purposes, and may seem so unhampered that men sometimes envy them, saying that they would like to be free as birds. Actually, of course, birds are not simply free to fly and sing—they *have* to fly and sing. Man also has to go through many motions in order to go on living, but he is the only animal that can deliberately choose and change his purposes, even to deciding not to go on living. Over the last five thousand years of his history he has enormously widened the range of his choices. In this view, freedom has been limited by stupidity and ignorance but more specifically by social constraints, the power of custom and convention. These induce *internal* constraints, which may appear as dutifulness or reverence, but may owe chiefly to inertia, superstition, insecurity, anxiety, or dread. We must therefore qualify the apparent freedom of primitive societies, which civilized men are also wont to envy in their harried or sentimental moods. The most easygoing primitives (such as the Stone Age Eskimos described by Stefansson) are free to consider relatively few possibilities and do relatively few things, but the great majority are hidebound by tribal custom. All have a severely limited range of self-determination, or power to decide for themselves what kind of selves they would like to be or become.

An immediate difficulty here is that internal constraints, as states of mind, are more intangible, elusive, and ambiguous than external constraints or positive abilities. To minimize this difficulty, some social analysts prefer Bertrand Russell's negative definition of freedom as "the absence of obstacles to the realization of desires," ruling out consideration of the nature of these desires. I am assuming that we may waive for the time being the question of the propriety or wisdom of the desires, but that we should take into consideration the range and openness of choice, the awareness of different possibilities, the desire to make choices—the *presence* of conditions helping to refine, extend, and enrich consciousness—as essential to the distinctive freedom that man is capable of, even though this gets him (and the analyst) into more trouble. Considering only "the absence of obstacles," no creature is freer than a well-fed, castrated household cat, and the freest man is the perfectly conditioned inhabitant of Huxley's Brave New World. A civilized man is conscious of richer possibilities than a South Seas islander, and as he seeks them is bound to face more obstacles; yet he alone is able to make his desires and his choices really his own. If he is a Shakespeare or a Beethoven, he may become aware of still more obstacles, lay himself wide open to frustration, but in his creativity he may know a godlike freedom. And for ordinary mortals this matter of the power and the range of conscious choice becomes more important as we approach our own society. An immense increase in power over the natural environment has created a multiplicity of choices, a wealth of means and opportunities for the realization of desire—and as many more potential obstacles, opportunities for waste, blunder, and frustration.

On this count ordinary Americans are again much freer than the masses of men throughout history, and potentially freer than ordinary Athenians in ancient Greece, than their ancestors on the rude frontier, or than their fathers in the strait-laced small town. But here we may not be at all sure. One reason is the growing conformism, the popular ideal of being "well adjusted" at any cost, with little idea of the possible costs. The conformism is due immediately to the constraints upon those seeking economic and social success, but it is due as well to consensus, a willing acceptance of such constraints. In their prosperity, many Americans seem content to think and to want what others tell them to. They display little desire to realize their own purposes, make individual choices beyond choices in the latest models. In the absence of serious obstacles to the realization of paltry desires, they may feel free because they feel complacent.

They bring up another complication—the basic distinction between subjective and objective freedom, or between *feeling* free and *being* free. It is not an absolute distinction. One who does not feel free is liable to impotence, however great his latent abilities and wide his actual opportunities; one who does feel free may exercise his powers more fully and effectively, however limited they be. Feelings are no less real for being subjective or scientifically disreputable, and they cannot be simply disregarded, since they influence the capacity to choose and carry out purposes. They are among the chief threats to freedom in the modern world, in which a vast collective power and mass have dwarfed the individual, and ever bigger organizations make men feel ever smaller.

Nevertheless I assume that we should look first to objective freedom—to the roughly observable conditions and powers rather than the infinite subjective experiences that flow from them. We can hope to answer with some assurance the question how free peoples actually were in the past. We might find it very hard to say how free they felt. And in any case feelings are not a trustworthy index to the state of freedom as I define it. Primitives may consider themselves free, or more precisely not feel unfree, because they are unconscious of the constraints we perceive. Although we cannot be sure of the state of mind of the illiterate peasant masses throughout history, their usual passivity suggests that they generally took their subjection for granted and did not feel deprived of the freedoms we take for granted; folklore gives little indication of a yearning for such freedom. When feelings are written into the record by civilized peoples, they as often lend themselves to an ironic as to a compassionate contemplation. Scribes proclaim the deathless glory and felicity of rotten empires on the verge of collapse. Priests give thanks to false gods for blessings won by human effort. Today the many Americans who get red in the face over the "creeping socialism that is destroying our freedom" remain as free as ever to voice their complaints, to vote the rascals out, to go about their increasingly profitable business, and to enjoy the highest standard of living in all history; while in pursuing success they may look to outsiders like the veriest slaves to business, and in enjoying it may respond like puppets to advertisers and publicity men.

Such ambiguities accentuate the complexity of the social condition, the tangle of variable, immeasurable factors that make it impossible to specify with precision the kinds and degrees of freedom. The awareness of such ambiguities also indicates the possibility of at least a partial detachment, a reasonably objective view of the conditions that make men feel as they do, and make it necessary to discount and supplement their feelings. And immediately it spots a primary source of confusion—the inveterate tendency to identify freedom with other goods. One seeking to adhere to a neutral, operational definition is obliged to spell out what he does *not* mean by freedom.

Dreaming of his beloved, the imprisoned poet sang:

> Stone walls do not a prison make,
> Nor iron bars a cage.

We may rejoice that he felt so; but then we must add prosaically that iron bars do make a cage, that only a poet who had known freedom could write this, and that he will be freer when he is outside the stone walls. As an ardent lover, he might then run afoul of John Milton:

> License they mean when they cry liberty,
> For who loves that must first be good and wise.

Prizing liberty, we may relish this lofty sentiment too; but again we must first acknowledge that liberty can be loved by sinners and fools, can run into "license." We must face up to such historical actualities as republican Florence in the Renaissance—the freest, most brilliantly creative city of the age, and one of the most licentious. To identify freedom and virtue promotes the understanding of neither.

As high-minded, and often as arbitrary, is the concept of "rational freedom" that philosophers have been fond of. "A free man," wrote Spinoza out of a tradition dating back to Plato, "is one who lives according to the dictate of reason alone." Human freedom does require a measure of rationality; a man governed by impulse or passion is obviously limited in his ability to choose his purposes; and it may be argued that no kind of freedom is more important than freedom from bondage to unconscious or irrational desire. Yet Spinoza was strictly defining a *wise* man—or more strictly a monster. Free men and free countries have never been governed by the dictate of reason alone. Philosophers have never agreed on the content of this dictate. Spinoza himself might be called a slave to his passion for utter rationality. The endless disagreement among the wise men may not clinch the right to be wrong, but at least it gives good reason to question any prescribed form of rationality. "If only rational freedom be allowed," Edgar Sheffield Brightman observed, "freedom ceases to be free and rationality ceases to be rational."

Another practical objection to such definitions is that they have commonly encouraged an indifference to seemingly unreasonable external constraints, in particular the condition of the masses of men. The last word in "rational freedom" is the Stoic ideal of freedom from all desire. "If once you swerve from this course," Epictetus warned, "you are a slave, you are a subject, you have become liable to hindrance and to compulsion." So indeed you have—freedom is always a risky business. The way of the Stoics could afford more tranquillity, to men in any condition of life; it was a "freedom" that even slaves could enjoy. But this is precisely the objection to it. A slave is not actually free, no matter how indifferent he may be to his chains. In spite of their ideal of universal brotherhood, most Stoics were content to accept the institution of slavery, though most slaves were not. Prizing above all the power to accept any lot, to "choose" whatever happened, the Stoics could ignore all constraints except desire itself, or their own desire to be imperturbable at any cost.

For similar reasons one may question the more common and attractive idea of "spiritual freedom," or specifically the Christian teaching, "In God's service is perfect freedom." This service can promote freedom in the ordinary sense of the word— *if* it is a free, conscious choice, and service of a God who encourages purposeful activity on earth, including free inquiry into his own purposes. Historically, however, the service of God has not always made for such freedom. Most men have served him out of unthinking habit, when not compulsion or fear. Those who seemed to be most intimately acquainted with his will gave different accounts of it, but typically they permitted men little latitude in choice. Martin Luther, who preached so eloquently the "spiritual liberty" of Christians, was as fiercely hostile to religious, intellectual, or political freedom. Only in recent centuries has God blessed the idea of political freedom, and more doubtfully of intellectual freedom. At its best, "spiritual freedom" is essentially subjective, the feeling of emancipation that may come through religious experience. A more precise word for it is peace of mind. If it brings freedom from anxiety, its essence is still service: obedience, submission, renunciation—"Not mine but Thy will be done." Such holiness may not be wholesome, but may come down to a surrender of human powers and purposes for the sake of freedom *from* freedom.

In general, the proponents of both rational and spiritual freedom have been inclined to agree that it means only the freedom to do what is right and good, by their own standards. What I mean by it is a state in which the individual may decide for himself what is right and good. It includes freedom of conscience, a kind of freedom that appeared late and intermittently in history, and that Lord Acton (himself a devout Catholic) made the very essence of freedom: "the assurance that every man shall be protected in doing what he believes to be his duty against the influence of authority and majorities, custom and opinion." And I have been stressing these objections to "true freedom" because those who know what it is naturally assume that all other good men will think and feel as they do, want the same good that they call freedom. At best, they confuse the actual social problem, which arises from the different kinds of freedom desired by different men, and the need of accommodating and adjusting these different desires. At worst, they tend to impose their standards of the right and good, and so to deny men actual freedom in thought and deed.

Western history is an endless illustration of such confusion and coercion. In Western thought a celebrated example is Hegel's pronouncement that "positive freedom" is achieved by an "utter obedience or complete abnegation of one's own opinion and reasonings," which meant specifically an utter obedience to the Prussian state. Only in being what the state wills us to be, added his English disciple Bosanquet, can we find freedom; and he concluded, "Thus it is that we can speak, without a contradiction, of being forced to be free." It is gratifying to a dialectician to be able to speak so, but it therefore becomes necessary to insist that this *is* a contradiction, compulsion is *not* freedom. For such philosophical double talk comes down to a hoary linguistic trick that today is a means of systematic, high-powered fraud—the trick of exploiting the emotional value of a word in order to sell some other idea. Insensibly it leads to the "Newspeak" of George Orwell: "Freedom is slavery."

All this is by no means to deny the intimate connection of freedom with questions of what is right and good. The power to choose one's own purposes leads naturally to the ideal of sovereignty over oneself, mastery of mean, irrational, self-defeating desires. When men claim the *right* to freedom, moreover, they must logically assume the moral obligation to respect the rights of others and the claims of the whole community, else there can be no effective freedom. They become more deeply indebted to the many other men, living and dead, who have upheld the ideal of freedom as an ethical principle. The very growth of freedom forces the questions of what is right and good, which ordinarily do not trouble primitive societies or most men in closed societies. Hence no student of freedom can ignore these questions, no matter how conscientiously he tries to refrain from moral judgment. He is obliged to consider its relation to such social needs as order and security, to such social ideals as justice and equality, to cultural or spiritual values in general. In the modern democracies, where common men have been freer to do as they please, he has to consider the questions raised by what they please to do; for the popular ends of freedom react upon the institutional means, and may confuse or obstruct the processes of democracy. I am merely assuming, once more, that one may hope to get a clearer view of such problems if one keeps one's eye on objective freedom, in the relatively neutral sense of my definition, and distinguishes the question of its nature from the question of its proper uses or ends.

Lest this definition seem arbitrary, I conclude with a restatement in terms of the categories made out by Mortimer Adler and his associates, from their exhaustive analysis of twenty-five centuries of thought on the idea of freedom. They found that all conceptions of it came down to variants on three basic definitions: *circumstantial* freedom of self-realization, or the ability of a man under favorable circumstances to act as he wishes for his own good as he sees it; *acquired* freedom of self-perfection, or the ability of a man through acquired virtue or wisdom to will or live as he ought in conformity to the moral law or an ideal befitting human nature; and *natural* freedom of self-determination, or the ability of a man to change his own character creatively by deciding for himself what he shall do or become. (The wording is Adler's.) Common to all the definitions are the idea of a positive ability and the idea of the "self" contrasted with some other, exempt from the power of others. Adler summarizes the underlying agreement as follows: "A man is free who has in himself the ability or power whereby he can make what he does his own action and what he achieves his own property."

Now I have emphasized this ability or power as distinctive of human freedom, beyond the ability of animals to carry out their instinctive purposes. My definition accordingly includes the idea of "natural" freedom, latent in all men by virtue of their powers of mind; but unlike many thinkers who have regarded such freedom as primary, I hold that the realization of the power of self-determination depends on circumstance or culture. My definition also includes the concept of "acquired" freedom, though in a broader sense and with important qualifications; for in most definitions this is the "rational" or "spiritual" freedom popular with philosophers. I believe it essential to conceive freedom as something that has been achieved and that can be increased, diminished, or lost. For similar reasons I object to definitions that limit it to a particular mode of self-perfection, and that slight when they do not exclude the common garden varieties of freedom. As Adler makes clear, most proponents of "acquired" freedom have held that it could be acquired only by a superior few.

As he perhaps does not make clear enough, most have been indifferent to social and political conditions that made it difficult or impossible for ordinary men to become masters of their faculties, to make their actions their own, or to achieve any perfection beyond complete obedience.

For a historian, the most important freedom is "circumstantial." It forces attention to the whole culture by which the self is molded, and thought about freedom is conditioned. One variant of it is political freedom, a major theme in Western history. Allied with this was the characteristic Western effort at social reform, the deliberate alteration of circumstance. But apart from such efforts I assume that for a society at large "circumstantial" freedom is essential to the other freedoms. However "natural," the freedom of self-determination has been rare or negligible in primitive societies, and among the illiterate masses of most civilized societies. If the "acquired" freedom of self-perfection may make a man superior to circumstance, its attainment initially requires the favorable circumstance of a high level of culture. The philosophers and saints who have preached such freedom had to preach it because it was beyond the ken of most men. The circumstances of civilization made possible their lofty ideal, and in most societies also made it attractive because there was little if any hope of more "circumstantial" freedom.[2]

[2] Adler has confined his study to Western thought, for reasons possibly parochial but still legitimate. In Eastern thought, from ancient Egypt to India and China, there has been little specific concern with freedom or effort to define it. Many of the wise and holy men never used

And so I think it may be well to stress at the end that the noble ideal of freedom involves the possibly ignoble idea of doing as one pleases, the irresponsible idea of doing things just for fun. As the old ex-slave said, he liked freedom because "there's a kind of looseness about it." Most of us cherish this looseness. As we acknowledge our obligations and our immense indebtedness to our fellows, recognize that "no man is an island," we still want an island of privacy, where we can sprawl and indulge our own sweet pleasure. If we are depressed by the growing conformism, we might cherish as well the stubbornness, even the cussedness of the ordinary man in resisting his superiors who are so sure that they know better than he what is good for him. "It is man's inherent willfulness that I would preserve," Learned Hand declared, "and in which I wish to set the stronghold of that Liberty I prize; that stone which social reformers have always rejected I would make the head of the corner." This willfulness can be very dangerous, needless to add. Still, it is in fact of the essence of human freedom. If it is ever extinguished in man, he may at last become a contented, well-behaved animal; but he will no longer be a free one.

---

the word. But Adler could find a great deal of Eastern thought to illustrate the concept of acquired freedom of self-perfection.

II.

The Nature of Man

THE POWER to choose and carry out his own purposes may be held the essential condition of man's claim to peculiar dignity and worth. This is a disputable claim, especially in view of the use he has made of this power in recent times. It raises further questions. Is man actually free to choose his own purposes? If so, is he fit for freedom? Does he really want to be independent? Such questions in turn force a broader, more fundamental one: What is the essential nature of man? Implicit in all ethical and political theory, as in all the higher religions, is some conception of human nature. Any serious thought about what is good for man logically requires some idea of what he is good for. And here is the beginning of a deeper confusion.

In our own tradition the oldest, most persistent definition of man—older than Plato—has split him in two, conceiving him as an immortal soul somehow imprisoned in flesh. Christian thought intensified this dualism, magnifying both the beast and the angel in man. He was a fallen creature, a cesspool of natural depravity; and he was nevertheless potentially fit for an eternity of bliss with his Heavenly Father, in whose image he had been created. Secular thinkers then seized upon either of his dual aspects as the fundamental truth about him. To Hobbes he was incorrigibly selfish and aggressive, always lusting after power, and could be made obedient only by fear. To the philosophers of the Enlightenment he was naturally good and potentially still better, perfectible by virtue of being a rational animal, and therefore deserving of freedom. In the last century he was studied much more intensively as history became a major interest and the new sciences of man got under way—psychology, sociology, anthropology. As a result we now have an immense body of knowledge, and a profounder confusion than ever before. Having gone through the mill of Darwin, Nietzsche, Marx, Freud, Pareto, and Dewey, looked into the mirror of Zola, Dostoyevsky, D. H. Lawrence, Joyce, Kafka, and Sartre, modern man may be forgiven some uncertainty about his being. And these radically different conceptions of human nature not only have as different theoretical consequences for the good life and the good society, but make some difference in man's actual behavior. Although the ordinary man has a certain toughness of spirit that enables him to resist his mentors, he wants to be "natural," and his common sense is a tissue of more or less unconscious theory about his nature. He may violently resent criticism of his self-image.

The confusion is not hopeless, however. Much of it is due to an insistence on strictly undemonstrable assumptions, such as man's possession of an immortal soul, and more especially to an arbitrary selection of some one potentiality of human nature as its "essence." The fact remains that we do have an immense body of reliable knowledge, in particular the advantage of historical and anthropological perspectives that make it fairly easy to discount the many oversimplified definitions of man. It is possible, I think, to reach an agreement upon some broad generalizations—not broad enough to include all the ideal possibilities cherished by many men, but adequate as premises for a study of human freedom, and even surprisingly helpful in avoiding common confusion. I am accordingly stating as objective truths, not mere hypotheses or articles of faith, the premises that man is a social animal, an animal with unique powers of mind, and therefore a culture-building animal. Through the development of culture, which long tended to obscure the individual, he eventually realized that he was also an animal with a distinctive capacity for individuality, or personality.

That he is an animal I take it is unquestioned. This is the body, the flesh, the beast in him that believers in his immortal destiny are the first to emphasize. With other animals he shares such basic drives as hunger and sex, such basic emotions as fear and rage, and all the physical limits on freedom. He can also enjoy sensations of physical well-being, take pleasure in his kinship with other forms of life, feel at home in the natural world. Everyone knows these elemental pleasures and pains of the flesh, the beginnings of good and evil, but lofty thinkers tend to slight them. They have often sought a freedom from all bodily desire, under the aegis of disembodied reason or spirit. Gratified by the thought that man cannot live on bread alone, they may forget that man cannot live without it, that untold millions have died for want of it, and that today most of the world's population still have to live without enough of it. They may see nothing very bad in bodily suffering, or even view health with some suspicion.

That man is a social animal should be as plain. In this respect he is still akin to the many other animals who live in flocks, herds, swarms, and schools, not to mention the highly developed insect societies. The "state of nature" is for man a social state if only because of the prolonged helplessness of the human infant. As far back as we can see him, in prehistoric caves, we find him living in groups; and as he emerges more clearly we see him differing from other animals in that he takes care not only of his young but his old, even his dead. Nowhere do we see the anarchic individualism, the endless war of all against all, that Hobbes pictured as his natural state, and Schopenhauer assumed was his most natural tendency. Looking to the unformed child—the little savage in our midst —we see him eager to learn all kinds of rules, and indeed to make them up.

Even so, many "realists" still assume that man is essentially an anti-social animal, an egotist whose oldest, deepest instincts are hostile to law and order. Such assumptions grew out of the traditional emphasis on the natural depravity of man, and grew more plausible in a highly competitive society devoted to the pursuit of wealth and power. They took on the appearance of scientific authority from evolutionary thought, with its early emphasis on the constant struggle for survival. They were confirmed by Freud, who saw a blind self-seeking and mutual antagonism as the primal drive in the unconscious, described conscience as "merely the dread of society," and regarded civilization as a ceaseless struggle against the state of nature. And there is plainly some truth in such views, which in complacent periods may be the truth that most needs to be said. Any parent knows that the human child is not a born angel, trailing clouds of glory, and that he likes to break rules too. The best friends of man have always known that he has selfish, egotistical, unsocial tendencies. From their different point of view champions of individual freedom have likewise assumed a basic hostility between the individual and society.

Yet the historical evidence overwhelmingly confirms the natural sociality of man. Almost all societies, from the most primitive to the most civilized, have emphasized duties much more than rights or liberties, and almost all their members have accepted these duties without protest. The inconstant creature feared by political philosophers has generally been constant in obedience, often submitting to what may strike us as wholly arbitrary, unnecessary constraints on his selfish interests. From the evolutionary point of view, the struggle for survival has been primarily a struggle between species, not individuals, and man has succeeded primarily by co-operating, not fighting with his fellows. Today we overlook the extraordinary extent of his co-operative behavior—co-operation required by organized competition—because it is less conspicuous and dramatic than competitive, aggressive behavior, or simply because we have come to take it for granted. If men are naturally antagonistic, as Freud believed, they have none the less succeeded so well in living together that the "abnormal" individual is the one who does not accept the constraints of the group. As for the champions of individual freedom, they are a rare type historically, and have rarely been popular. Their ardor testifies that the impulse to accept and obey is much stronger than the impulse to rebel.

To define man as a social animal is therefore no more idealistic than to call a bee a social insect. His sociality does indeed provide a natural basis for idealism, in that his "selfish" interests always include the interests of some other selves, the need of warmth and affection. It involves a natural sympathy and natural piety, as in the care of his dead, which may flower in ideals of our common humanity, or of "natural rights"; it is not based primarily on anything so uncertain as enlightened self-interest. But this is also to say that it is generally un-reasoned. Another word for man's constancy is inertia, an-other word for sociality is herd instinct. Today the common word for it is conformism. It can be said that most men are not intelligent enough to pursue their own interests, not cou-rageous enough to have self-esteem. It cannot be said that sociality means simple fraternity. Men have never loved their neighbors as themselves, still less all other men. Their natural loyalty to their own group has always tended to make them suspicious of outsiders, hostile to other groups. Societies have most clearly exhibited the selfishness and aggressiveness that have been attributed to the anti-social nature of man, and conflicts between them have been fiercer because their members have usually been willing to sacrifice their personal interests to the cause, even to die for the group.

Hence "realists" may still find sufficient propensity to evil, or, if they prefer, Original Sin. My point is merely that it is not realistic to describe man as an animal who has been driven into society in defiance of his natural instincts, and who can be held there only by force or through fear. The life of the lone wolf is no more natural to him than the life of the hermit. In the tensions of our own society, which has set up an ideal of individualism, encouraged competition in education and recreation as well as business, demanded an unprecedented extent of co-operation, achieved an unprecedented degree of organization, and provided an unprecedented wealth of opportunity for self-realization and for maladjustment, it is both more tempting and more misleading to assume an inveterate hostility between the individual and society. The rugged individualism that alarms some critics and the lack of individuality that depresses others are alike social products. Today, as in the past, society dominates the great majority of its members. From its domination arise the major issues of freedom.

Also beyond dispute, and a source of incessant dispute, are the powers of mind that most clearly distinguish man from all other animals. In physiological terms, he has by all odds the most complex, elaborate nervous system, centered in the brain, which gives him abilities different not only in degree but in kind from the intelligence displayed by other "higher" animals. Some animals can solve problems, and many—down to chickens, fish, and cockroaches—can learn from experience after a fashion; only man can consciously remember what he learns, conceptualize it, put it into words, teach it to his young. With his power of reasoning he has as distinctive capacities of imagination, sensibility, and insight. His consciousness is a stream of perceptions, intuitions, feelings, fantasies, impulses, thoughts unimaginably different from whatever goes on in an animal's mind. As Dewey observed, the idiomatic meanings of *mind* give a more comprehensive, just idea of its nature than do the formal definitions of logicians and most psychologists. I have states of mind, good and bad; I make up or change my mind; I keep things on it, and put it on matters; I may lose it, though without losing my consciousness or my nervous system; I may be of two minds or half a mind; I mind my step, mind my own business; I mind my children and make them mind me; I mind if I am deprived of my freedom. Ultimately *mind* involves the vague but real power of the "human spirit," which seeks the good, the true, and the beautiful, and inspires the exalted idea of soul. Immediately it also involves less agreeable possibilities. Because man can make conscious choices, he may make unintelligent, ridiculous, even fatal choices. No other animal is so stupid as a human fool.

Only with drastic qualifications, then, can man be defined as a "rational animal." His experience is much broader and richer, untidier and wilder, than a pure rationalist would have it. His basic impulses—to eat, to make love, to rest, or simply to go on living—are all non-rational; his behavior is often positively irrational, more "brutal" than the purely instinctive

behavior of brutes. Still, this is to judge him by rational standards, and finally to emphasize his capacity for rational thought
and behavior. The capacity is most apparent in the practical
activities by which he has gained power over the natural environment, but it is also implicit in his co-operation with his
fellows. In every known society he has recognized the principle
of *ought* by assuming responsibilities, committing himself to
duties at the expense of his own sweet pleasure. In every society he is *held* responsible, punished when he does what he
ought not to do. In civilized societies those who insist on the
basic irrationality of man still lay down the law for him and
insist that he obey it, stay in his place. Such demands on him
are grounds for the assumption that he ought to be treated as
potentially a rational animal, not a brute. If thought does not
make the whole dignity of man, as Pascal declared, his capacity for thought in the broadest sense remains the clearest
index of his humanity, the basis of his claims to dignity and
worth—and so to the right of freedom.

Together with his sociality, it has made him a culture-
building animal. Whereas every generation of apes begins and
ends where the last generation did, without benefit of the wisdom of their ancestors, the children of men begin by acquiring
the knowledge, skills, and arts accumulated over the countless
generations before them. With these they absorb the whole
way of life of the fathers. And here the most pertinent fact
is the most conspicuous one in an anthropological and historical view—the extraordinary diversity of the world's cultures. It makes plain what is never plain to men in any given

society. Man lives primarily in a symbolical world, a world of his own creation. Always set in a natural environment, always compelled to deal with natural forces, he gets from his society all his ruling ideas about the nature of the world and how to deal with it. His basic "reality" is not physical but cultural, spiritual. He begins learning metaphysics in his cradle. If he becomes a professional metaphysician, he is more likely to lose sight of the cultural facts of life.

So we might pause to consider the familiar term *nature,* which is as ambiguous and confusing as any in the language. His mentors have often told man to live "in accordance with Nature," finding in Nature the source of his duties and more recently of his rights. So capitalized, the word means something like God and enjoins some ethical code, but it only veils the mystery of the nature and the will of God; what code it enjoins will depend upon the speaker and his culture. Another common meaning of *nature,* the unbaptized universe and everything in it, is no more helpful; in this sense nothing can be contrary to nature, whatever man chooses to do is a natural event in the universal show. In the more common sense of the external world, everything in the universe apart from man, *nature* becomes more misleading. It may now mean a bountiful provider, a haven from care, a playfield, a bloody battleground, a constant menace, an enemy of all man's works—a spectacle beautiful or grim, serene or wild, majestic or awful; but if the familiar counsel to "follow nature" means to follow instincts, live like other animals, it is positively inhuman so far as it is feasible at all. At best, the simple idea of going back to nature simply obscures the real problem, the ultimate concern of all philosophy and religion—the problem of what is the good life for man, a creature for whom all kinds of behavior, from loving to killing, are on the face of it "natural."

Immediately it obscures the basic fact that "human" nature is a second nature—largely made by man, not simply born in him. Whatever instincts he is born with may be cultivated, blended, modified, diverted, or suppressed in so many different ways that they appear to be bare potentialities, raw materials for the unconscious artistry of culture. The ruling drive in one society may be a matter of indifference to another, a positive abnormality to still another. Hence when men grew self-conscious and sophisticated enough to inquire into their nature, their culture suggested the answers; and the endless confusion began. In the Western world the answers grew more diverse as society grew more complex and unsettled, but the confusion was intensified by the nature of thinkers—their common craving for simplicity, the One instead of the Many. Bent on reducing the many apparent motives to a single ruling motive, they have variously defined it as self-interest, the will to power, sexual drive, the craving for freedom, the craving for security. Today many still overlook the plain implications of the diversity of human culture, the radically different ways of life that alike seem natural to men brought up in them. The most solemn injunctions about the needs of Man usually spring from the parochial needs of some contemporaries.

We can still make out basic uniformities, however, else we could not speak of *man* at all. Men everywhere have a common structure, common needs and desires, common capacities; everywhere they have to cope with the same exigencies of birth, growth, sex, toil, suffering, and death. Their common mortality is the strongest reminder that their common humanity is not a mere ideal, but a fact. Hence even the apparent artificialities of culture are to some extent natural outgrowths of common potentialities. A man might think it patently unnatural for women to paint their fingernails and toenails—were it not that women have always been doing such things, as far back as we can see; and men have seemed no less interested in improving on God's or nature's handiwork. The universal vanity involves the common possession of an aesthetic sense. The rise of civilization brought ways of life that would seem still more artificial, except that all along the most natural behavior for man was evidently not to follow nature but to master it, adapt it to his own purposes. Finally, in the Greek world, there emerged the ideal of culture in the high sense of the word, the conscious cultivation of human nature and its capacities for the pursuit of truth, goodness, and beauty. With this emerged the choicest and the most troublesome product of civilization—the self-conscious individual. The dignity of man, wrote G. H. Mead, consists in the fact that when he calls upon himself he finds himself at home.

In the Western world this fortunate caller has dared as never before, dared even to stand alone. He has made extreme claims for himself. He has demanded political freedom, to participate in the determination of the group purposes, the means to the common good; individual freedom within the state to carry out his private purposes, realize his own good; freedom against the state, to assure his inalienable rights. He has proclaimed the supreme value of personality, even when he no longer identifies it with an immortal soul. He has declared that the individual must be regarded as an end in himself—the state exists only to serve him.

He is therefore apt to forget that he is a parvenu in history. Whatever consciousness other animals may have is certainly not self-consciousness. If man in primitive societies ever thinks of calling upon himself, he seldom finds his *self;* he has little consciousness of individuality apart from his group, and less of rights against it. In most civilizations it never occurred to men to think of consciousness as intrinsically individual, or of individuality as the quintessence of human nature. Hence, too, this parvenu has been liable to extravagance. His rise in the world has inspired an atomic individualism that represents society as a kind of artificial bond, created by self-conscious individuals for the sake of enlightened self-interest, with the policeman on the corner to keep watch on the unenlightened; a rugged individualism that makes self-interest a moral principle, and tends to narrow and impoverish individuality by an exclusive devotion to economic ends; a romantic individualism, or cult of genius, that conceives individuality as the sum or essence of what distinguishes or separates a man from his fellows, excluding all that unites them. It becomes necessary to repeat the commonplace that man is a social animal. His very consciousness is a social product; he becomes aware of himself only through his relations with other selves. Likewise his individuality can be realized only in a society, and a rich one achieved only in a highly developed society. The gospel of individualism is itself a product of a free society.

Today, however, students of society are most likely to ignore the individual or to deny his importance. Anthropologists have generally treated him as a mere carrier of culture, which has its own laws and seems to carry on by itself. Historians concentrate on the deep, involuntary processes of social change, and in reacting against the Hero theories of history they often explicitly minimize the role of individuals. Sociologists likewise concentrate on impersonal processes that may appear to be automatic. Some have declared that the individual is only a cell in the social organism, and that as a creature having an independent reality he is a "discredited hypothesis"; more have buried him in statistical abstractions like the "average man"—a monster who has 2½ children. Many students of the life and work of even the great men of the past study them primarily as products of their age or examples of major tendencies. It appears that the deepest meaning of a play by Shakespeare or Racine must be the thought or feeling of most ordinary men of their time.

I therefore judge that what most needs to be stressed today is the reality and the unique importance of the individual. Physiologically, man is the most highly individualized of animals, and as he developed his latent powers of mind he would naturally become more so. Individual differences have made a great deal of difference, even if during most of his history man has put little stock in any except military prowess; for whatever progress he has made must ultimately be traced to them. Knowing nothing about the origins of culture, we can still be confident that it was a very gradual, unplanned growth, not the conscious creation of farsighted individuals; yet it did depend upon the discoveries and inventions of exceptional individuals. "Society" did not dream up the idea of pots and looms and wheels. With the rise of civilization came a massive growth that may look involuntary and certainly was beyond the understanding and control of the individual; yet it involved more conscious doing and making, in which gifted individuals had freer play for creative achievement. If society now made possible a Socrates, a Confucius, an Archimedes, a Christ, it still cannot claim full credit for their greatness—it produced chiefly ordinary men. And as we begin to trace the growth of freedom, it becomes more necessary to keep an eye on the individual. Whether or not we regard him as an end in himself, the freedom of a society is meaningful only as it is exercised by individuals, and can be observed only in their behavior.

A more debatable issue, however, is raised by the democratic tradition that has made so much of the individual and done so much for him. Eighteenth-century philosophers who helped to shape this tradition commonly assumed that man is a rational animal who has not only a natural right to freedom but a natural passion for it. History hardly supports this congenial idea: until recently the masses of men have not demanded such a right or displayed such a passion. History suggests rather that Dostoyevsky's Grand Inquisitor may have been right. For the great majority of man, he said, the freedom of choice offered by Christ is an intolerable burden; what they want and need first of all is bread, and then "miracle, mystery, and authority." Now psychologists and sociologists are asserting that the ruling passion of man is for security. Hitler may have been sincere when he proclaimed himself an emancipator: "Providence has ordained that I should be the greatest liberator of humanity. I am freeing man from the demands of a freedom and personal independence that only a few can sustain."

This is an open question. If civilization is not destroyed by an atomic war, it is perhaps the most fundamental question of the future. At this point I should remark only that my premises allow for the measure of freedom that man has actually achieved, and for the possibility that sociologists and psychologists may be no more infallible than Hitler's providence.

Simply as an animal, man does not like to be caged. One instinct that the human infant clearly is born with is a resentment of confinement, and as he grows up he normally likes to keep active, explore and master the world about him. As a social animal man looks somewhat tamer than he may like to think, but he still displays some independent spirit in home, shop, and village. As an animal with powers of mind he has a natural curiosity and likes to use his head, if not always on what his teachers try to pound into him. As a builder of culture he imprisons himself but also learns how to exercise his creative abilities, express himself. If the earliest recorded expressions of his spirit indicate little or no positive yearning for freedom, they often do indicate a resentment of unfreedom. In many languages "bonds" are a symbol of evil or misfortune, while many myths, legends, and fairy tales suggest a covert rebellion against the symbols of convention and authority, in the defeat or discomfiture of king, giant, father, or stepmother. If civilized men became conditioned to such institutions as slavery, with the approval of their gods, there is little evidence that the slaves themselves welcomed it, plenty of evidence that they lamented it; whenever enabled to purchase or recover their freedom they usually did so. Today the passion for security leads few men to welcome the perfect security of a jail.

On the record, freedom has not been the ruling passion of mankind; yet once men have known any kind or degree of it, they have seldom knowingly given it up. Inasmuch as almost all of us cherish our freedom it would seem unreasonable and inhuman to declare dogmatically that men are not fit for it, or to oppose efforts to fit them for it. Aware of the infinite variety of culture, we know that it is natural for men to accept as right and necessary whatever way of life they have been brought up in; but our knowledge of the different possibilities of life also gives us grounds for deploring many ways that men have accepted out of ignorance. We can at least argue that is is better for them to be conscious of their actual potentialities, their latent powers of choice. We are then arguing for the need of some freedom in mind and spirit. But we are brought back to an as yet unproved assumption—that man actually does possess such freedom,

III.

The Reality of Freedom

ALTHOUGH we may train Fido to behave as we see fit, and call him a good dog when he obeys or punish him when he does not, we do not consider him moral or immoral, still less reprove him for his affairs with other dogs. We assume that his behavior is governed by instinct and conditioned reflexes, not by conscious purposes of his own. The assumption that man is able to choose his purposes and to will his deeds is the premise of all moral judgment. It is an absolutely essential premise, and is in fact implicit in all social behavior. Whatever they believe, men feel and act as if they are more or less responsible for their deeds. They always feel that they deserve credit for their good deeds; if they often try to escape blame for their bad ones, they are still prone to feelings of guilt or remorse; and they advise, warn, threaten, or beg their fellows, always assuming that they may get others to change their minds. Yet the actuality of human freedom remains a live issue. It has been denied by many eminent men, on both religious and scientific grounds. And disbelief in it may also make a real difference in behavior.

In the conviction that man was utterly dependent upon the

will or whim of the gods, many early peoples devoted a great deal of anxious effort to pampering or placating the gods, and to ascertaining their will. With Christianity the denial of human freedom became more explicit. St. Paul introduced the doctrine of predestination; Luther and Calvin among others more emphatically rejected the presumptuous idea of free will. Given an omnipotent, omniscient God, this is indeed a logical conclusion. The Almighty must be in complete control of his creation, completely aware of everything his creatures would be up to. How could man in any real sense surprise or disappoint him, much less defy his will? Today predestination is a dead dogma in Christendom, but something of its logic survives: churchmen are again reminding men of their utter dependence upon the grace of God, condemning the sinful belief that man could progress by his own unaided efforts. In orthodox Islam predestination remains a basic dogma.

Scientific determinism followed as logically from the materialistic, mechanistic premises of classical physics. If the behavior of every molecule is determined by mechanical laws, and man is composed of molecules, then his behavior is determined by such laws; there is no apparent room in a clockwork universe for a free human spirit, meddling with the works in unpredictable ways. Many thinkers accordingly agreed with Taine that what men call virtue and vice are merely chemical products, like sugar and vitriol. And while twentieth-century physics operates on different premises, the weight of scientific thought remains deterministic. Scientists naturally look for uniformities, fixities, necessities. In the labo-

ratory most still concentrate on mechanical or invariable processes. In the social sciences they still distrust such concepts
as purpose and value, which do not lend themselves to direct
observation, measurement, and controlled experiment. They
study man as a product of his heredity and environment, concentrate on the forces that condition his behavior and make
up his alleged mind. If few thinkers today assert an absolute
determinism, a great deal of influential thought is colored by
attitudes and beliefs that tend to discourage or discredit the
idea of free, purposeful activity.

In particular many are now disposed to believe that *collective* behavior, and therefore human history, are governed
by impersonal forces beyond human control. We have grown
much more aware of the deep, involuntary processes of social
change, the unintended results of all social and political action.
Nobody planned the Industrial Revolution, for instance. If
Francis Bacon and a few others foresaw the technological possibilities opened up by science, nobody foresaw the immensely
intricate society that has resulted from the exploitation of these
possibilities—a society that we are still trying to understand
and to manage. In this effort we have also grown more aware
that thought never keeps abreast of social change; men are
always behind the history that has already been made, and
that may therefore seem to make itself. Looking back, we can
often see a kind of remorseless logic, as in the invariable fate
of empire and the invariable failure of men to learn from it.
Trying to look ahead, we may see a similar logic in the ir-
reversible tendencies of recent history, as in the advance of

science and technology. We cannot undo the work of the Industrial Revolution, cannot give up the knowledge and the power we might prefer to do without. As a society we are absolutely dependent upon our machines, and upon the ever more complex social machinery necessary to make and run them. For all such reasons we hear much of the "laws" of history: laws that may assure a happy ending, as in the class-less society of Marx, or a tragic ending, as in Spengler's drama of invariable cycles of growth and decay, but in either case do not permit man to choose his future. Short of such his-torical predestination, many men feel that the race has lost control of its destiny, if it ever had any.

Now there is no gainsaying all that we have learned about the physical, physiological, psychological, and social determi-nants of human behavior. Yet there is no human necessity of gainsaying it, or reason to be simply distressed by it. One who believes that man is in some sense a free agent, and hopes that collectively he is still free to make his history, should be the first to welcome all such knowledge. It is valuable knowledge precisely because man can then do something about it, just as he acquired it by his own determination. Having discovered natural laws, he can bend them to his own purposes, as he has triumphantly done through science and technology. Once aware of conditioned reflexes, the drives of the unconscious, the mechanisms of heredity, the compulsions of custom, the tyranny of the past, he can hope to be no longer wholly at their mercy. Early American behaviorists gave the most curi-ous proof of his effective freedom: insisting that his so-called mental activity was absolutely conditioned by mechanical processes—and also insisting that they could so condition a youngster as to make of him whatever they had a mind to.

How man can be free in a lawful world may be a metaphysical mystery (though no less mysterious than how he could get his illusion of freedom if his behavior were completely determined). The empirical fact remains that he is able to do a great many things to suit his own purposes. The plain source of this ability is his highly developed brain; intelligence itself is a power of deliberate choice. On biological grounds his powers of mind remain mysterious because they enable him to defy the strongest and most essential of instincts, self-preservation; but again the empirical fact remains that he can determine even to kill himself. If we cannot absolutely prove man's freedom, we can at least find sound reasons for our living belief.

On religious grounds, the reason why predestination is a dead dogma in Christendom is as clear as its inescapable logic. It makes pointless the central doctrine of the Redemption: Christ was crucified only to save those who were predestined to be saved. When coupled with the idea of eternal rewards and punishments, it becomes shockingly unjust. The religious spirit demands that God be good; his goodness is more essential than his omnipotence and omniscience, for which there is no absolute logical necessity.[1] And, despite their logic, those

[1] William James and many other religious thinkers have been able to conceive, as Zoroaster and Plato did, a limited deity, responsible only for the good in the universe. This leaves open the question where all

who preached the doctrine of predestination or denied free will were always involved in a logical contradiction by the mere fact of their preaching. From Paul and Mohammed to Luther and Calvin, they continued to expound, exhort, and upbraid as if men could save themselves. They insisted that men shoulder the blame for their evil ways, which God had preordained.

On scientific grounds, the problem of human freedom in a lawful universe has been confused by common-sense notions of law and causation. A scientific law is a statement of certain uniform sequences, as of the regular falling of apples in accordance with the law of gravitation. It is not a universal commandment, not a description of a force that *makes* the apples fall, not a final explanation of *why* all the apples fall. The cause assigned to a sequence of events is in any case selective, never the whole or the "real" cause. If a chicken is run over by an automobile, its death may be attributed to the laws of mechanics, the nature of living organisms, the stupidity of chickens, the carelessness of the driver, the sins of American automobile designers, or the curse of an industrial society. A similar set of causes may be assigned to all human behavior, from the most mechanical to the seemingly spontaneous. "Free" activity need not mean activity that is uncaused or unaffected by the environment. If it did, freedom would be a nightmare in which nobody could understand or count on

the evil comes from, but the mystery is less troublesome than the mystery of why a perfect God created a woefully imperfect universe.

the behavior of others, everybody could enjoy only the freedom of lunatics.

The essential idea is that some human actions are not simply mechanical, wholly predetermined, absolutely predictable, but are to some extent self-determined and unpredictable. Although this "self" is always conditioned by its whole past, in a given culture, it still has live options and may say yes or no. If behavior becomes broadly more predictable when a man has character and acts on principle, his decisions are then more clearly his own; and there is still a margin for judgment, ingenuity, imagination—the brilliant decision. We may predict that a poet will keep on writing poetry because of an inner compulsion, but we cannot possibly predict his next happy phrase or far-fetched metaphor.

Let us consider even routine behavior, as of a man who gets up in the morning when his alarm clock goes off. The ringing of the clock is a mechanical, automatic event. It was predetermined by the designer of the clock, through creative powers of mind, and then by this man's setting the alarm. His own behavior involves both reflexes and reflection. He set it out of habit because he had to get up, go to work, make his living—because of necessities that limit his freedom, but also help him to achieve his living purposes. Even so, he might decide not to get up, instead to lie in bed a while—possibly to chuck the whole business. In either case his behavior is not causeless. Call it rational or irrational, one can find reasons for it. The point remains that once he is awake he is not behaving like an automaton. Unlike other animals, he is not merely following instincts either, but is thinking ahead, exercising some conscious judgment.[2]

It may help to remember this individual as we consider collective behavior, the deep social processes of which he is mostly unconscious and often the victim. The Industrial Revolution —unforeseen, unplanned—was nevertheless man-made. It came about through the conscious, purposeful, creative activity of a great many individuals, applying the discoveries of other individual scientists—not of "science." Its unintended results by no means disprove human freedom; they prove only the limits of human foresight. One reason why men failed to foresee them is that it was an unprecedented development, without parallel in other civilizations. That it now looks like a logical, lawful development does not imply that it was inevitable or automatic, any more than is the understandable behavior of individuals. As a great historical "movement" it led Henry Adams and others to look for laws comparable to the laws of motion in physics, but it was essentially different from physical motion; the most significant goings on were within

---

[2] I am not invoking the Principle of Indeterminacy in modern physics, which has been eagerly misinterpreted by defenders of spiritual values. This principle applies to our knowledge of electrons, not necessarily to their behavior. It means that we cannot know at once both the location and the velocity of an electron. It does not mean that the electron is a free agent with a will of its own; the behavior of crowds of electrons in a chunk of lead can be determined and predicted for all chemical purposes. Man himself would be in a bad way if the electrons in his body were lawless or fancy-free. In general, the point of the revolution in modern physics is not that it proves the reality of human freedom or clinches human values, but that it leaves philosophical room for these values in a universe no longer conceived in purely mechanistic terms.

the minds of men, in societies that did not move. It illustrates no fixed "law" of history. For none of the comprehensive laws yet proposed are strictly scientific laws, upon which historians have agreed or can agree. All amount to rough generalizations, based upon underlying similarities in social need and response, recurrent tendencies or probabilities. None are statements of invariable relations, applying uniformly to all past events and making possible certain prediction of future events. None are binding upon the individual, either as leader or as follower.

The Industrial Revolution also emphasizes a major factor in history that alone makes certain prediction impossible—the factor of knowledge. This revolution resulted directly from an advance in science and technology, and while we may anticipate a continued advance, we cannot foretell the knowledge men will have in the future, and with it the power at their disposal. Thus Marx could hardly foresee the hydrogen bombs that make his disciples less eager to have a world revolution. Meanwhile Marx illustrates a further uncertainty introduced by the very effort to predict the future. His prediction that capitalism is inevitably doomed has helped to inspire a mighty collective effort to assure its doom. It has also inspired efforts to reform capitalism, control the economic forces that he assumed would have free play. The determination of the Communists may very possibly determine the future; but capitalism as described by Marx, and as still lauded by American conservatives, has long since ceased to exist.

Hence Marx is perhaps the most conspicuous example in modern history of another power minimized in his theory of economic determinism—the power of conscious ideas and ideals. Many other thinkers now tend to treat ideas and ideals much as he did, as primarily reflections of the social process, rationalizations of the event, at most as symptoms rather than effective causes. There is no question that they do arise out of the social process. Yet they do not arise spontaneously, all by themselves; they come out of the heads of individuals. The social process is complicated enough to produce a whole spectrum of thought, from revolutionary to reactionary. In a strictly deterministic view it is never too clear how men can be either revolutionaries or reactionaries—*against* their times, or the society that "produced" them; but in any case the social process forces men to make choices in ideas and ideals. So men all over the world are now being forced to choose between the varieties of Communism and democracy, or to devise some intermediate system that may better suit their own tradition. The compulsion at once limits and challenges their effective freedom—the freedom of reason, imagination, and good will, in combating the necessities imposed by blind selfishness and the tyranny of the past.

It would seem plain, then, that conscious ideas and ideals are both cause and effect of the social process, in no simple one-to-one relation but a continuous interrelation, in ways difficult to determine because they are not uniform, automatic, or predetermined. To believers in freedom, Communism should make as plain that a belief in the power of ideas and ideals is not pure or simple idealism. The ideas that have most obviously and deeply moved men have always been questionable, sometimes demonstrably false or absurd. The more questionable they are, the more likely they are to inspire fanaticism; men are wont to die most willingly for the Hitlers. But men have always fought and died for "the things that are not seen," or that are seen only in symbols of flag or Cross. The practical spirit that makes many business and political leaders in America underrate the power of ideals may make them look like hopeless visionaries themselves—dreamers devoted to business as usual, things as they are, in a world that is nevertheless revolutionary. The issue between Communism and democracy may be decided immediately by military power, the new weapons resulting from new ideas in science and technology. In the long run the decisive factor may well be the power of the ideal of freedom.

Meanwhile there remains another paradox. While the growth of an immense collective power has made the individual liable to feel more impotent than ever before, this power is effectively at the disposal of a few individuals, in particular the leaders of America and Russia. Upon decisions made by these very few depends the fate of our civilization. Any strictly deterministic theory founders on this appalling fact; but so may the human race.

IV.

The Ends of Freedom

THE VALUE of freedom might be called self-evident. It is a good in itself, known immediately by all men in the good feeling of being free, realized more fully when it has been lost. Many have held it to be the supreme good, and have fought and died in the belief that it is as precious as life itself. Recent history might bear out the familiar warning: if men regard it as merely a useful means, or as less important than security, wealth, comfort, or any other earthly good, they are pretty sure to lose their freedom, and then likely to lose whatever they prize more. Yet freedom cannot actually be a sufficient end in itself, even for those willing to die for it. It is not necessarily a good thing; few rejoice when an escaped criminal or madman regains his freedom. At best men cannot be simply free or simply happy in being free—they must always be doing something with their freedom, employing it to some purpose. As they become freer, have more choice in ends, their most difficult problems begin.

Although it has seldom had high philosophical or religious sanction, the most apparent universal end sought by man is happiness. All men normally want to be happy; no man consciously sets unhappiness as his life goal; no society considers suffering a good in itself. But in its most popular form, simple contentment, happiness can hardly serve as a measure of freedom. Primitives and illiterates may well be as contented as citizens of a free society, and morons even more so; all might envy the contentment of the household cat. Civilization itself has been aptly defined by Whitehead as "a program for discontent." The program got under way in prehistoric times with the invention of tools—inventions that are commonly thought of as basic necessities but were in fact luxuries, since men had got along without them for many thousands of years. "The most civilized people," Lord Raglan observed, "are those who regard as necessities the largest number of luxuries"—and who therefore lay themselves open to more discontent. Among the later luxuries, and the clearest signs of discontent, were philosophy and the higher religions, which told man where his "true" happiness lay and typically denounced most other luxuries.

All these spontaneous, unforced developments suggest, however, a familiar principle. The natural end for man—the source of civilization and the only clear justification of it—is the realization of his distinctive potentialities as an animal with a power of mind or conscious life. It is the development of his capacities for knowing, feeling, making, striving; the extension, enrichment, and refinement of consciousness. Self-realization in this broad sense embraces the other traditional ends of freedom made out by Mortimer Adler and his associates. It implies a power of self-determination, and requires the development of this power if the self is fully to realize its possibilities. It includes the various possible ideals of self-perfection, though again without assuming a fixed, given human nature. A man may determine to fulfill himself in the way of Confucius, Epicurus, Aurelius, St. Francis, Spinoza, or Kierkegaard; but I assume that he is freer when he is aware of various possible ways, and of the values and the limitations of each. In any case, happiness is the by-product of self-realization.

So too is unhappiness; and so we cannot absolutely prove our living assumption that it is good to be a conscious animal. Many great teachers, beginning with Buddha, have denied that life on earth is worthwhile. Nevertheless they have generally sought to lessen unhappiness, or in effect to make life more worthwhile; and we can point to elementary goods that may make it so. Almost all men know such basic goods as physical well-being, with rest and play; comradeliness and love, or satisfying human relations; the enjoyment of beauty; the satisfaction of the creative impulse, to make or grow things; the satisfaction of natural curiosity, to find out about things. That these goods cannot be strictly demonstrated need not be disheartening. Any logical justification of them would be an argument that they are good for something else (such as the dreary argument that sports mold character, or that art must serve morality); whereas their essence is that they are absolute goods, good in themselves, good for their own sake. Once experienced, they are known to be good and require no demonstration. Men will knowingly sacrifice them only for the sake of some consuming passion or some "higher" good, such as salvation in a life to come.

These "higher" goods are in general the values developed by civilization—moral, aesthetic, intellectual, religious. As it is with them that the difficult problems begin, we might first note that they are still essentially natural as outgrowths of the elementary goods. The fine arts, philosophy, science, ethical and religious idealism—all may get remote from common sense and the common life, but all stem from the interests and needs of a curious, creative, social animal. They may be called higher goods for the purely empirical reason that they give deeper, richer satisfactions. The ordinary practical man pays at least lip service to them as "the finer things in life." They also have deep elemental connections with one another, indicated in such common expressions as an honest piece of work, a beautiful deed, an elegant theory, a love of truth. Because it is easy to talk loosely about the higher goods, hard to define them, impossible to reach complete agreement on them, it is the more necessary to keep in mind the all-important distinctions they refer to. There can be no self-realization worth speaking of without the realization that some kinds of pleasurable experience are more valuable than others, some goods more desirable than others, some selves better than others. Freedom only heightens the importance of these choices, which for most men are largely unconscious or ready-made even though all want to get the most out of life.

Unhappily, the devotees of the higher goods are themselves apt to obscure the natural origins and social uses of these goods, and to complicate the problem of choice by a jealous exclusiveness. In theory, the natural ideal for man would seem to be a full, rounded development of all his powers, an approach to the wholeness and harmony implicit in the intimate connections of the good, the true, and the beautiful. In practice, most men naturally cultivate their particular interests and gifts, and may best realize their powers by intense concentration. The single-minded or lopsided man—the pure artist, scientist, scholar, saint—is as common a type as the well-rounded man, and may be more admirable. The trouble remains that such men are likely to consider their own interests self-sufficient or supreme, to become not only indifferent but hostile to other major interests, and so to become narrow on principle. Devotees of "rational" or "spiritual" freedom, who are especially disposed to sacrifice ordinary goods to their version of the highest good, make it still harder to approach the ideal of wholeness and harmony by commonly insisting on a radical dualism, not only distinguishing but separating higher from lower in such antitheses as reason and passion, body and soul. Like the official custodians of spiritual values, they are also given to insisting that all goods have the proper metaphysical or religious credentials. Lofty thought has seldom been satisfied with any ideal not certified as absolute, universal, eternal truth.

Historically viewed, such truths always look like the temporal ideals of a particular society, when not of a particular thinker. Although they are usually underwritten by God, his testimonial also manifestly depends upon the society and the thinker. The whole history of thought testifies that men do not have certain knowledge in these high matters, and that their claims to certainty grow more impassioned because they cannot conclusively validate them. It provides no absolute standard by which to judge among the conflicting versions of absolute truth. It displays the remarkable boldness of the human mind, and a less remarkable fear of the unknown. A student of freedom may believe, as Lord Acton did, that he knows the essential truth about God and man's destiny; but like Lord Acton he is obliged to record that such convictions have often worked to curtail or deny freedom of thought and conscience.

As one who professes no knowledge of the ultimate or no intimacy with deity, I am adhering to a principle of relativity and final uncertainty, in the conviction that local, temporal, relative goods may still be real and sufficient goods. This principle is not a flat denial of the "transcendent truths" beyond human experience on earth that many thinkers have somehow got hold of, for there are always possibilities transcending ordinary experience and certain knowledge. But it does declare that what cannot be publicly tested is not certainly true, and that a recognition of the limitations of the human mind is not necessarily a defiance of the divine mind or a betrayal of the cosmos. In particular, it is as I conceive it a positive moral principle, of humility, tolerance, liberality, breadth. While it makes choices freer, it by no means evades the problem of judgment or makes choice easier. Given the different ways of life exemplified by Buddha, Confucius, Socrates, and Christ, for example, I have no means and feel no necessity of declaring that any one is absolutely the best way; yet I do judge that all are honorable ways, and I would say flatly that any one is better than the way of Mammon or Moloch, Hitler or Stalin.

This implies some principle of judgment beyond a mere acceptance of the historical fact of relativity. The most insistent cultural relativists, indeed, are actually committed to certain liberal values, beginning with tolerance. They say that we should respect all cultures, though it would be as logical to say that we should respect none of them. They condemn the illiberality and cultural conceit that are virtually universal. Nor do they really believe that such common historical practices as tyranny, slavery, and torture are merely the different ways of other cultures, which we have no right to judge, or that they are merely poor policy. They believe that these are evil things. So almost all of us believe in our hearts that it is simply *not right* to enslave men, to torture men—our feeling is absolutist. And the basic principle implied in such common judgments, it seems to me, is a respect for the human personality, or more broadly a reverence for life. It is an outgrowth of the natural sympathy of a conscious, social animal for his fellows. It is connected with the idea of sacredness found in all religions: an idea everywhere associated with the supernatural, but in the higher religions associated as well with the human spirit that seeks to know, honor, and serve the God, and in Christianity most specifically with the human personality, in the name of soul.

Most religious thinkers accordingly assert that any naturalistic principle is hopelessly inadequate for a proper understanding of man, and still more so as a ground for idealism—for the effort to preserve the sanctity of personality, or more especially the ideals of a free society. They point to the brutal disrespect for life in the modern secular world as proof that we can maintain these ideals only on a religious basis, in the name of absolute truths certified by God. This is another open question, to which I shall return. Here I should say only that it is a much more complicated question than supernaturalists usually make out. A brutal disrespect for life has never been prevented by the commands of God, even when backed by threats of eternal torture in hell (which incidentally do not suggest a reverence for life or promote the idea of the sanctity of personality). Historically, authoritarian regimes have almost invariably rested on absolutist principles and claimed the sanction of deity. Absolutism can justify almost any faith, but can justify intolerance and coercion more readily than freedom. If skepticism may open the door to ruthlessness, it can hardly provide a sanction for any absolute authority.

For purposes of analysis, at least, the naturalist or humanist has some clear advantages. Supernaturalists look odd when they charge that he makes man the measure of all things, ultimately makes judgment merely subjective; for they themselves make the whole universe conform to man's desires, even to declaring that it was created just for his sake, and they provide no objective means of testing the truth of their claims. Lacking the authority of the Absolute, the naturalist may judge more objectively in the light of tested knowledge and shared experience. He may discern more readily the effects of supernatural hopes and fears on earthly freedom. He may consider more freely the various possible ends of freedom.

Still another open question brings us closer to the necessary commitments of a free society. In considering its ends, John Stuart Mill noted a broad but historically fundamental distinction between the active and the passive type of man: the one seeking to bend circumstances to his own will, to struggle against evils, to improve his earthly condition, and so promoting the values of enterprise, initiative, independence of spirit; the other seeking to adapt himself to circumstances, to bear any lot, and so promoting the values of patience, obedience, resignation, humility. To most Westerners today it may seem self-evident that the active type of man and life is superior. But as Mill pointed out, most of the great moral and religious teachers of mankind have held up the passive ideal, as Christ himself did in the Sermon on the Mount. In most civilized societies this has been the accepted ideal.

On naturalistic grounds, I see no way of declaring that either type is absolutely, necessarily superior. Surely there is wisdom in the passive ideal. It has helped millions to endure a hard lot with fortitude and some measure of grace; given all the catastrophes in history, and the threat of worse catastrophes to come, it might be the best wisdom for the majority of men, in particular the many contemporaries who appear to crave peace of mind. In its higher manifestations—of contemplation, composure, self-denial, non-attachment—it is a mode of self-knowledge and self-realization that may yield a deep or even rich contentment. As surely the passive ideal cannot be called unnatural for man. It should remind us that the "human nature" we hear so much about is in fact the nature of Western man, or more precisely of some Western men, and is rather different from the nature of both the Indian peasant and the Hindu mystic.

Yet it is undeniable that the active type of man has promoted the growth of freedom, as in his discontent he led the rise of civilization. William James remarked the fantastically unnecessary needs of man, in the satisfaction of which the race has established itself; and he added, "Prune down his extravagance, sober him, and you undo him." You hardly undo him, considering the longevity of Eastern civilizations; but at least the ideal of a free, full realization of human potentialities is also natural for a conscious, creative animal. One may add with Mill that the active ideal is positively superior in one respect, that an energetic spirit can more easily learn patience than a passive spirit can acquire energy. Likewise a free society can better accommodate diverse modes of self-realization, including the wisdom of passivity. At any rate, a believer in democracy should be conscious that he is committed to a faith in the active ideal. The values of passivity can be fully realized under authoritarian or despotic regimes, and historically have flourished under such regimes. All arguments for the superiority of democracy finally rest on the assumption that it is better to encourage and enable ordinary men to participate freely in the active effort to promote the common good, and not to accept poverty, want, disease, or any remediable social ills as the law of life or the will of God.

Similarly the ideal of active self-realization commits one to a belief in the value of individuality. The self that appears in all the traditional definitions of freedom, and that has the power of making its actions its own, can realize this power only by becoming conscious of itself as an individual. If thinkers devoted to the "acquired freedom of self-perfection" have generally demanded that a man rise above individual desires, or have held that the "true self" is selfless, their ideal can be attained only by individuals with uncommon powers. Granted that individuality is a social product, still society does not automatically breed it—much more obviously it breeds pressures to uniformity. Granted the impersonal processes and unplanned developments in history, still all the great creations of man were the creations of great men—they were never merely the products of history. We are likely to forget the multiple roles that even the ordinary individual is able to assume in the community, and the latent abilities he can never fully develop; for when he is most successful or socially useful, he still might have been a better carpenter, athlete, musician, mechanic, or dozen other things. In any case the truth remains that only by being an individual with a mind and character of his own can a man fully realize his humanity. And only through the exercise of free, conscious, responsible choice can he become such an individual.

All in all, self-realization may be called the primary meaning of the evolution of man, and of the history of civilization. In this view human history has been a progress, however slow, wayward, and erratic. By the same token, it has not been progress pure and simple. A finer, fuller consciousness is no guarantee of wisdom, virtue, holiness, happiness, or any other end. We are led to the inescapable costs of freedom.

V.

The Costs of Freedom

ALTHOUGH God, by Christian definition, represents "infinite freedom," in a sense man is even freer. God must be perfectly good and perfectly rational—in effect he is required to obey St. Thomas Aquinas. Man can act on whim, fancy, impulse. He is free to be a fool or a devil as well as a saint. He can defy the commandments of God himself. But in this view freedom is the cross that he *must* bear.

Tradition has it that the major costs of freedom, especially political freedom, are disorder and strife. These are real costs, and were conspicuous enough in the ancient Greek cities that set up the conscious ideal of freedom. Tradition has magnified them, however. Disorder and strife have been common to all great societies; they have flourished under autocracy, aristocracy, theocracy, and every other form of government. Traditionalists customarily simplify and falsify the past in the light of their characteristic ideals of stability and certainty, which men have never achieved and can never hope to achieve— short of the death they fear. To realize the full costs of freedom we need to go much deeper, and first into the elementary.

We begin with the age-old paradoxes, the fantastic nature

of the only self-conscious animal, the only one who can love himself and hate himself, try to know himself and persistently deceive himself. Thought makes the whole dignity of man, as Pascal said; and it is the Primal Curse, the source of all his peculiar woes, the reason why he must ever live dangerously. His power of choice means the perpetual possibility of foolish or fatal choices. Grown more conscious, it means livelier possibilities of doubt, disquiet, disharmony, discontent. Exercised successfully, it still creates as many problems as it solves, and finally settles nothing. Every new satisfaction becomes a new need, new source of dissatisfaction. And the higher goods exact higher costs, involve deeper contradictions. The pursuit of truth, goodness, and beauty has entailed a more acute consciousness of error, evil, and ugliness, and has created more perverse and dangerous forms of them. Monsters have been glorified by art, deified by religion, and today armed by science.

Hence every major historic advance in freedom has *ipso facto* created new problems, including new threats to freedom. Increasing mastery of the natural environment brought increasing dependence on the social environment, at once more security and more insecurity. As the group grew more resourceful, the individual grew less self-sufficient. With the coming of civilization, a vast increase in the collective power, most men became subjects and might feel impotent. The extension and refinement of consciousness led to a fuller, keener consciousness of necessity and morality, of man's dependence on nature or the undependable gods, of his insignificance in the cosmos. The growth of freedom in thought brought on more complications. For the group it meant first of all a threat to the social order, further possibilities of disharmony and disruption; for the individual it meant more awareness of possibility and of constraint, more opportunity for self-realization and for frustration. The self-conscious individual with a mind of his own, who may be considered the glory of civilization, may epitomize its costs. Able to contribute much more to the community than its unthinking members, he is also more apt to disregard it, exploit it, or defy it, for reasons selfish or idealistic; he is always liable to become a victim of it; and he may suffer still more from alienation, aloneness, the cross of self-knowledge.

So one can go on, indefinitely, tiresomely—as I shall throughout this study. Meanwhile I should stress the costs of freedom as not only a fact but a methodological principle. In general, it counsels us to think in terms of both-and instead of either-or and is-nothing-but; to remember that if it is all one in the end, it is first always two or more; or simply to remember that history is indeed as complex as almost everybody says it is. More specifically, it calls attention to the natural ambiguities and incongruities of all culture, a man-made world in which man becomes "cabin'd, cribbed, confined"; of all institutions, which are necessary to carry out collective purposes and as necessarily involve routines that may thwart intelligent action; of all social orders and creeds, which must ignore or suppress some possibilities in order to realize others, and like individuals always have the defects of their virtues. It prepares us for the ironies of great creative achievement, which then tends to limit or discourage creativity by fixing standards and styles, and of revolutionary movements, which always tend to go too far and therefore never go far enough. It sets the terms of historical judgment as at best partial successes, relative goods, mixed fruits. In efforts to judge our own situation, it sets the problem of emphasis—what most needs to be said to a given group at a given time; and it therefore guarantees that one will always be misunderstood and misjudged.

But another reason for stressing the inevitable costs of freedom is to preserve the values and the real gains in freedom. The popular faith in progress as a kind of automatic movement onward and upward, continuing by itself as everybody goes about his private business, has bred a complacence that under pressure easily gives way to panickiness, baring a radical ingratitude for civil liberties that were hard won. On the other hand, a revulsion against this naïve faith has made it too easy to ridicule the whole idea of progress, to dwell on the steady succession of failures in the past and disasters in the present, and to forget the positive goods that have been realized and retained in spite of all the failures. The historic record has always been mixed: a record not of constant, uniform advance but at best of the fitful realization of new possibilities, sporadic bursts of creativity; and the most brilliant bursts have always been destructive of traditional values, often fatal to the society that produced them, as they were to ancient Athens and Renaissance Italy. Such progress as man has made, and may still make, is guaranteed by no known law of nature, history, or God. It has always been uncertain and must always remain so, if man is in any sense free to make his history. The immediate conditions of uncertainty—tension, imbalance, instability, insecurity, disharmony, conflict—are the essential conditions of possibility and aspiration. We cannot appreciate the extraordinary adventure in freedom unless we remember that it has always been a precarious adventure, always demanded resolute, arduous effort. The full worth of liberty is known only to those who know its full costs. Its price remains eternal vigilance.

Part Two

The Basic Cultural Factors

VI.

The State

MOST men now consider freedom primarily a political issue, having to do with the state rather than with culture. The broader view of it that I consider necessary implies some distinction between the state and society as a whole. This is a distinction that the ancient Greeks and Romans failed to make, and that Western thinkers have often ignored or even denied; yet it is an essential one, and essentially factual—not merely verbal or ideal. The neglect of it was a major limitation of classical political thought, and is a major source of confusion in modern thought.

As defined in the dictionary, a *society* is a recognizable group sharing common interests and aims, or a common culture. It is not a sharply defined group except in small primitive societies. When it is called a *people* or a *nation,* it takes on political implications that narrow its meaning. A society may endure after a nation collapses or falls to another people; or nations may belong to a greater society, a civilization. Such larger groups are much less homogeneous, much more blurred at the edges, but they may still be called societies in so far as they have a recognizable common tradition, or as their members are conscious of belonging to them, have a sense of community. *Community* would perhaps be a better term than *society* in that it stresses more the common interests and the essential unity. With either term, however, I am stressing the aspect of totality. A society or community embraces all the significant interests and activities of its members. It is broader than the anthropological term *culture,* which refers more to what is shared and may obscure the people—the individuals who make up the group and transmit the culture.

A *state* is a group formally organized to secure law and order, through a system of government and a body of officials. Primitive societies, ruled by custom or unwritten law, usually have only the rudiments of a state, as in a chieftain or a council of elders. In civilized societies the state is typically the largest and most powerful organization. Yet it is still only a part of society, a means to the communal ends; it does not embrace all the interests and activities of the group. Modern democratic states have explicitly limited its domain, walling it off from the home and the church, drawing up bills of rights that give the individual freedom from it or rights against it. Totalitarian states have sought to dominate the entire society, and have in fact controlled business, religion, literature, education, and recreation to an extent that the most despotic states of the past never attempted; but even so they do not and could not control all social activity. No organization could possibly assign every man his mate, his occupation, his friends, his interests, his choice in food, dress, and fun. No more could an ardent patriot devote himself heart and soul to the state alone, except over brief periods. The most powerful totalitarian state is still not in fact identical with the society. Its people may hope to survive the overthrow of the state.

Now oppressive as the state may be, it is clearly a necessity in any large, civilized society. Only a Marxist visionary can believe that it will ever "wither away." This side of Utopia, the state is the primary social organization, as the essential means to the law, order, and security on which all other social goods depend. Hence men everywhere have recognized its right to make extreme demands on the individual, even to the sacrifice of his life in time of war, and have generally regarded treason as the worst of crimes. Likewise they have everywhere given the state authority to use force in compelling obedience to law and maintaining order. In Max Weber's words, the state has "a monopoly of the legitimate use of force"; it is properly the strongest power in a society. And because power is now an ugly word, and always a dangerous thing, we should realize that it is not simply an evil thing. There is no virtue in a feeble state. Power does not merely or invariably corrupt, else there is no hope for man. It may make a leader more sober and responsible; historically it has been used to preserve and extend as well as to crush freedom. This side of Utopia, only authority backed by power can secure rights and liberties. Americans still tend to regard the state as a necessary evil, but they have come around to taking fuller advantage of its necessary power in order to promote their effective freedom, by such measures as public education and unemployment relief.

Even law has obscured the fact that the state may give

people much more than it takes away. The common definition of freedom as merely the absence of external constraints leads men to assume that law, like authority, is a natural enemy of freedom, and every new law a further encroachment on it. Every law does indeed restrict the freedom of some men; burglars are seriously inconvenienced by laws against theft. Still, men can never be free without it. Constraints are as indispensable for positive freedom as red lights are for safe traffic. Especially in the Western world, law has been the very source of civil and political liberty. As the Greeks rose to freedom, they set the ideal as a government by laws instead of government by men. The Romans passed on the basic tradition of freedom under law. By law the English gradually set limits to the power of their monarchs and secured their liberties. The men who made the American Revolution, like those who made the English Revolution, had characteristically a profound respect for law. Its importance was only emphasized by the doctrine of the "natural rights" of man, for the overwhelming majority of men had never enjoyed these rights; they became natural only when embodied in law. Needless to add, laws can be stupid, unnecessary, unjust, tyrannical. One who contemplates the proceedings in our legislatures and our courts might at times find more attractive the Confucian ideal of a harmonious social order in which law is unnecessary. Nevertheless law remains at the heart of the Western tradition of freedom; and if its power finally rests on the consent of men, it also rests on the coercive power of the state.

The state has still other ideal aspects. Its rise in the Western world provided a degree of equality in citizenship as a right by birth, instead of by feudal privilege. It has helped to inspire the growth of richly diversified national cultures, which in turn have stimulated the exceptional creativity of Western civilization. It has been a major means to the establishment of wider communities, increased mutual trust among much larger bodies of men than Plato and Aristotle thought could be governed well. In recent times the nation-state has become a symbol of freedom, the right of all peoples to self-determination. Scores of new states are now represented in the United Nations, seeking to work out their own destiny.

Their jealousies, however, recall us to ugly realities. The worship of the nation-state—a distinctively Western development that has now swept all over the world, and that is nevertheless too often considered "just human nature"—is the plainest threat to the efforts at world order and peace upon which the survival of the human race may depend. It is patently stronger than the devotion of Americans to ideals of freedom, or of Russians to the ideals of Communism. Given this modern worship, and the historical record of nationalism, I take it that what most needs to be emphasized is the historic confusion between state and society.

Mussolini stated it most baldly: "All for the State; nothing outside the State; nothing against the State." Even before Hegel, political philosophers repeatedly fell into such confusion. "The *social* compact," Rousseau declared, "gives the body *politic* absolute power over all its members" (italics mine); from this fiction he could go on more easily to his idea of "forcing" men to be free. "Society is indeed a contract," wrote Edmund Burke; and in the next sentence he substituted the state, winding up with his famous definition of the state as "a partnership in all science; a partnership in all art; a partnership in every virtue, and in all perfection"—all sprung from "the great primeval contract of eternal society." We do not in fact owe all science, art, virtue, and perfection to the state, which is neither primeval nor eternal. It only orders—it does not create. At any given moment the state looks less sacred because it is necessarily represented by a government: a body of mortal officials who like as not are grievously deficient in science, art, virtue, and perfection, and at best are not to be trusted with "absolute power" over all members of the community. In sociological terms, a society may be regarded as something like an organism, since it is not a deliberate organization, still less a mechanism, and has a kind of organic unity. A state is more like an organization, a government is essentially a mechanism.

Granted this factual distinction between state and society, the immediate problem is to determine the actual sovereignty exercised by any given state: the domains of communal interest and activity that it seeks to regulate or control, the domains that it leaves free. This may be difficult to determine because its control of major interests, such as business, religion, art, and learning, has usually been partial, indirect, or unofficial, due mostly to its prestige as the largest organization in the society and as the chief symbol of unity. It may be less despotic than it looks because it does not exercise power it has in theory; it may be more despotic than its laws suggest because its practice differs from its ideal theory. In constitutional or democratic states this problem takes on a philosophical cast. They have more consciously raised the question of where on principle to draw the lines, the limits of state sovereignty. Thus Americans have long been arguing over the extent to which the state should be permitted to enter and regulate business; whereas they have long agreed that it may rightly intrude on so private a domain as the upbringing of children, by making education compulsory. We may assume that such debates will go on indefinitely, with thinkers on all sides of every question. A conscious debate of such questions nevertheless represents an advance toward freedom.

A related problem is the legitimacy of the great power in any case exercised by the state. All civilized societies have implicitly recognized some distinction between society and state by efforts to make their sovereign a legitimate authority; the almost universal solution until recent centuries was the idea that the monarch got his authority from the gods. In democratic states men have had to think harder about this problem. If they might enlist the authority of God for their constitution, they could hardly do so for their elected rulers; hence the source of legitimacy became "the will of the people," or in practice law. In their concern over the legality or constitutionality of a given measure, they often neglect the question of its wisdom, its bearing on effective freedom or social justice. But this concern again marks an advance in freedom.

Another way of sizing up a state on this score is its policy toward other organizations within society. Any large society embraces many smaller communities, beginning with the family and the village, that may more clearly exemplify the essence of community, or realize Burke's ideal of partnership. Civilized societies also include organizations deliberately formed. In early civilizations they were few in number and limited in independence. The relatively liberal Roman Empire was still suspicious of them; it discouraged or tried to suppress all but the most harmless recreational and religious associations. Totalitarian states today naturally keep all organizations of consequence under state control. Democratic states, on the other hand, are distinguished by the multiplicity of relatively independent organizations—political parties, churches, universities, clubs, labor unions, chambers of commerce, professional associations, societies for the promotion or prevention of one thing or another. By their freedom such organizations accordingly create political problems, even when they do not become powerful enough to threaten the state. They may promote divergent interests, conflicting loyalties, sometimes a bitter factionalism. In the democracies they have earned the disagreeable name of pressure groups. But for better or worse they emphasize the basic distinction between society and state —a distinction still likely to be forgotten by professional patriots in the democracies.[1]

[1] A magniloquent example was provided by Senator Henry Cabot Lodge (once a historian) when he led the fight against American entry into the League of Nations. "I can never be anything but an American," he chanted, "and I must think of the United States first. . . . I have never had but one allegiance—I cannot divide it now." This undiluted,

These associations also bring us back to the individual. They help to maintain a pluralistic society, offsetting the power of the state, defending the rights and furthering the interests of the individual. They are mostly associations that he can freely join, and through which he may more fully express and realize himself. In the modern world they may help him escape the feeling of impotence that the massive state is likely to induce. They are not, however, ideal means to such ends. Large organizations always tend to become bureaucratic hierarchies, which may in turn threaten the freedom of the individual; he now needs protection against corporations and unions too. The private association, like the small town, may breed narrowness, exclusiveness, hostility to the independent spirit. The individual may join to escape himself or to lose himself, because he is fearful of independence or incapable of it. The rise of the "organization man" and the popular modes of "togetherness," not to mention the mass movements of Fascism and Naziism, should make it clear that community too is not a sufficient end in itself, nor any more than the state necessarily a means to freedom.

For some sociologists the ideal appears to be a stable, well-integrated society whose members are well adjusted. A student

undivided American was presumably a Christian too, and if so owed his primary allegiance to God. He was certainly a Republican, who sometimes appeared to think of his party first. He had loyalties as well to his family, to friends and colleagues, to Boston and Harvard, to assorted societies. As a member of the Senate he was different from most 100 per cent Americans, who spend 99 per cent of their time in business and social activities; but even so the Senate is an exclusive club, notorious for its jealousy of its privileges and private interests.

of freedom must be concerned about how a society is integrated and what kind of life its people are adjusted to. He might not welcome the stability and unity of Huxley's Brave New World. I assume that society is as much an abstraction as the state, and that the goods flowing from both should be looked for in the condition of individuals.

VII.

Technology and Commerce

IN *Progress and Power,* Carl Becker began with a question forced by the appalling disasters of our time: "What, if anything, may be said on behalf of the human race?" As a historian he knew that the race had paid little attention to the liberal values he cherished, but he found it helpful to take a very long view. Half a million years or so ago man was cousin and companion of the apes; now he puts the apes in the zoo. If he ran into his ancestor *Pithecanthropus* he would put the old man there too, and be amused by him for a simple reason: *Pithecanthropus* would be inside the cage, he himself outside. Man has acquired power. The key to human progress is the ugly word *power*.

It has thoroughly earned its evil reputation. Long before it brought on the appalling disasters of our time, ever since the beginnings of civilization, power has been the locus of man's worst problems. Yet we cannot hope to deal intelligently with these problems unless we recognize the supreme necessity of power, the plain reasons why there is no virtue in impotence. Only through acquiring power over his environment has man been able to realize his humanity, or whatever divinity may be in him. He has always cherished it. For thousands of years he sought to acquire it by magical means, as today he may still resort to prayer, but all the time he was gaining more actual power by his own discoveries and inventions; and he has clung to every gain. His history has been a steady accumulation of technical skills. The modern man on the street owes countless items of his food, his dress, his household goods, to as many peoples all over the world, most of whom he has never heard of, and some of whom never saw or dreamed of a street. The clearest progress that man has made has been in and through technology.

As a material progress, this too has come to seem evil, or at least somewhat disreputable. But it has involved an intellectual progress as well, a growth of durable knowledge. The result of intelligence, the expansion of power led to an expansion of intelligence: directly in organization and management, more extensive co-operation, more systematic pooling of labor and skill; indirectly through the leisure for intellectual pursuits provided by increasing abundance. Freed from material cares, the vulgar necessity of working with their hands, thinkers would in time become supercilious toward the "base mechanic arts," and others would learn to scorn the material wealth and power that are indispensable to civilization. They would forget all that the fine arts themselves owed to technology—not only architecture but sculpture, musical instruments, metalwork, stained glass, oil painting, the printing press, and photography. Histories of technology would not be written until this century.

In other words, the growth of power has been a growth of freedom—freedom from want, above all freedom *to* want, to choose and do. The acquisition of power is the clearest proof of the empirical reality of man's freedom. Necessity is not in fact the mother of invention. None of man's inventions were necessities, since he had got along without all of them for many thousands of years; and the neediest peoples today are generally the least inventive. Freedom is the mother of invention. So it may be called the mother of necessity too—the new necessities arising from the realization of new possibilities.

From the growth of technology followed the growth of commerce, another vulgar activity that has been a major factor in the growth of freedom. As Whitehead observed, commerce is a civilizing influence in that it promotes intercourse by persuasion instead of force. It is an essentially rational activity that puts a high premium on intelligence, if also on a low order of cunning; it requires calculation, foresight, resourcefulness. As a speculative activity in both senses of the word, it fosters a spirit of enterprise and adventure. It leads to a trade in knowledge and ideas, an exchange of cultural as well as material goods. It creates a larger world in which men are potentially freer from bondage to custom. There is no plainer example of its stimulus than the ancient Greeks, who in time learned to look down on commerce but first rose and flourished on it; they developed their brilliant culture in seaports, borrowing extensively from the learning and the arts of the more ancient peoples with whom they traded. As striking an example is Western civilization, in which an energetic bourgeoisie spearheaded the major developments: the growth of medieval free towns, the Renaissance, the discovery of America, the Protestant Reformation, the rise of science, the rise of democracy, the Industrial Revolution. The motives of commerce are basically materialistic, selfish, often sordid; but we must entertain the probability that it has contributed substantially more to the growth and spread of freedom than has religion.

This is by no means an invariable connection, however. Almost all civilized peoples have traded extensively, yet failed to develop free societies. Economic interests breed conflict, which has often resulted in the use of force again and the subjection of masses of men; the slave trade was long one of the most lucrative. Economic enterprise does not automatically beget freedom of mind or spirit. A business class is also inclined to conservatism, narrowness of interest, shortsightedness; the limitations of its mentality as well as its morality help to explain the relatively low social status it has enjoyed in all civilizations before our own. As the ruling class in our world it has not been distinguished for political wisdom or liberality. It fought every social reform now generally accepted, including some that proved to be in its own interests. It has narrowed and confused the issues of freedom by its gospel that economic freedom is the most fundamental, the very heart and soul of the American Way. It has mostly been indifferent to the civil liberties that are more clearly essential for the protection of the individual and the realization of individuality.

So it brings us back to the obvious dangers of power. The advance in technology that made civilization possible led immediately to the growth of political power, creating the problems that man has had to wrestle with ever since; for most men it meant subjection, less freedom than neolithic barbarians had enjoyed. The Industrial Revolution that made possible a machine civilization has magnified all the old problems and created new ones, even apart from the new weapons. In totalitarian countries rulers have not only a frightful military power, but through the mass media an unprecedented power over the minds of their subjects. In America an immense power is willy-nilly exercised by appointed bodies like the Defense Department and the Atomic Energy Commission, operating on secret information denied the rest of us, making without public debate such crucial decisions as whether or not to develop hydrogen bombs; while the powers of the mass media are exploited by private interests for private gain, immediately by specialists in the art of hidden persuasion or psychological assault. Producers and performers—the men with creative ability—are themselves often denied free, spontaneous, meaningful creativity as they are obliged to cater to the tastes of a mass public, or at least what advertising agencies decide those tastes are. Engineers are made to design automobiles with fins, and even top executives may feel obliged to manufacture the monsters.

In general, the tremendous expansion of power achieved through modern technology, together with the considerably less spectacular expansion of intelligence in the management of the social and political problems it has created, is the clearest illustration of the costs of freedom. It is less clear an illustration of the values of freedom. Material wealth and power remain indispensable means to the good life, and now open up possibilities such as men hardly dreamed of in the past; yet they are only means, and they always tend to obscure the ends. The type of "practical" man who dominates the modern world is almost by definition a man concerned only with means (though at that he is likely to be an ignoramus in science, the basic means—a Secretary of Defense who knows only that basic research "is when you don't know what you're doing"). In a world of machines men are apt to think as well as work mechanically. The wondrous possibilities are still live, the hitherto undreamed-of choices are still open; but they put man's powers of intelligent choice to a test more severe and more urgent than ever before.

VIII.

Religion

AS I noted earlier, many thinkers hold that Christianity is the fountainhead of Western ideals of freedom and democracy, and insist that only on a religious basis can we hope to maintain these ideals. Other thinkers see religion as a relic of primitive fear of the unknown, "the sum of scruples that interfere with the free exercise of human faculties," or even a calculated opiate for the masses, "a device for keeping people quiet while skinning them." Given so ancient, universal, enduring a power in human culture, one might expect the truth to lie somewhere between these extremes, and not to be simple or single. It is no less complex because the issue here is not the metaphysical question of the truth of religion, but only the empirical question of its effects on freedom. For the empirical reality is not religion—it is a multiplicity of diverse religions, in which each of the major ones embraces almost as much diversity of belief and behavior. Christianity has been the most diverse, from the outset splitting into sects that have multiplied into hundreds, and within its major Western sects undergoing profound changes. Most true believers today entertain beliefs that would have made them candidates for burning in the Middle Ages or in Calvin's Geneva.

The burnings, however, suggest an elementary distinction that can cut out much of the confusion. Broadly speaking, there is *ideal* religion, as represented by the founders of the higher religions and the great prophets, saints, and mystics; and there is *historic* religion, as represented by established churches and the often low manifestations of popular belief and behavior. They are connected, of course, but they are different enough so that an outside observer might not always deduce one from the other, and Jesus or Buddha might be bewildered by the worship in churches bearing their name. Those who exalt religion as "man's highest aspiration" and those who attack it as vulgar superstition or tyranny over mind are usually talking about different things.

Now one can only speak broadly about *ideal* religion, which has not been uniform or uniformly sublime. Although the teachings of the great founders are often unclear or uncertain, they certainly differ in some fundamental respects; Buddha seems to have been an atheist, Confucius something of an agnostic; and apostles and saints have sanctioned some beliefs that may strike us as unideal or even revolting.[1] Nevertheless we can make out basic similarities in the higher religions, more readily by contrast with the primitive nature

[1] Women in particular had reason to deplore the teachings of St. Paul, among others. Their status was generally higher in the early civilizations, before the rise of the higher religions and of philosophy made them a dangerous distraction from the spiritual pursuits of men.

religions before them, that entitle them to be called "higher."
All freed the human spirit for loftier aspirations. They rescued
man from his obsession with food and phallus by spiritualiz-
ing the powers to which he was subject, making them more
amenable to his ideal purposes. They gave him "immortal
longings," a vision of the Good beyond the flux of earthly
things. If the "spiritual freedom" they offered him was primarily subjective, not in my view the essence of human freedom, it was a mode of self-realization that cannot be
disregarded by anyone who respects the human spirit. The
higher religions did much to inculcate such respect, without
which no freedom can be secure. Generally they asserted principles of spiritual equality and personal responsibility that
implied the dignity and worth of the individual, and especially
in Christianity came to support his claim to rights.

It is difficult to do justice to such contributions because
they come down to platitudes, ideas now simply taken for
granted, and are less prominent than the shortcomings of religion. It is therefore well to remember that in their beginnings the higher religions were subversive, revolutionary
movements, undermining worldly or priestly authority. They
periodically inspired other such movements because their essential spirit was a quest of the Good. They are still potentially
subversive because of another idea they made commonplace
—that God demands worship by righteousness instead of by
rites. They preached a disinterested love, which makes for
freedom of spirit. With the higher religions the service of God
ceased to be mere servility. Men of all faiths might agree with

Berdyaev: "God is always in freedom, never in necessity, always in personality, never in the world whole."

Still, this is strictly an unorthodox view, not in fact widely accepted; and it brings us back to the familiar ambiguities. The founders and their apostles were mostly indifferent not only to political freedom but to the values of civilization, or to humanistic uses of freedom.[2] They were devoted to the supernatural and otherworldly, at considerable expense of natural, worldly interests. In liberating man from bondage to nature, they also tended to alienate him from the natural world, to lessen his confidence in his natural powers of intelligence, and to subject him to a supreme power that was potentially more tyrannical than nature—God is always an autocrat, heaven never a republic. In offering man higher hopes, they deprived him of other hopes, in effect declared that religion is his only hope. Often they taught that natural desire is evil, or at least more evil than suffering and pain. The great religious teachers have mostly offered man freedom *from* anxiety or spiritual want, seldom freedom *to* choose and carry out his earthly purposes.

They have also tended to create anxiety, as saints have often testified. By their very loftiness the higher religions may induce a sense of man's unworthiness, which in Christianity especially has appeared as a strong sense of guilt or sin. This may in turn induce a wholesome humility, even saintliness; or

---

[2] Confucius is a conspicuous exception to this and most of the generalizations that follow. But for this reason his primarily ethical, humanistic teaching is often denied the name of religion.

it may induce misanthropy, even hatred. "One was well-minded to understand holy writ," said Pascal, "when one hated oneself." One who hates himself is disposed to hate others—as Pascal said all men did "by nature." Here is one apparent reason why Christianity has inspired more positive hatred than has any other of the higher religions. (It may put a somewhat better face on the task of the American clergy, the difficulty lamented by one minister of "preaching the good news of a Savior to people who for the most part have no real sense of sin.") Short of hatred, a sense of unworthiness or sin is unlikely to inspire a struggle for more earthly freedom. Saints have rarely if ever crusaded for freedom. (And again one may be less depressed by the thought that America has produced no saints.) Self-denial led many a holy man to deny the rights of other men to realize themselves in other ways.

All such tendencies to discourage the ideal of freedom have been carried much further by *historic* religion. As necessarily worldly institutions, established churches invariably debase the teachings of the founder; their characteristic stock in trade has been "miracle, mystery, and authority," including a formalism and legalism that the founders were wont to denounce. They are naturally conservative institutions, bent on preserving old ways and their own vested interests. High priests have seldom welcomed new knowledge or new aspiration, any basic departure from traditional practice and belief. While insisting that the universe never leaves man alone, they have typically been hostile or at best indifferent to efforts to substitute rational for magical or prayerful ways of dealing with it. The great founders and prophets spoke "from the heart," with an impassioned, often unreasoned conviction; their ministers, speaking from holy writ, followed suit by appealing to the heart, but made simple credulity still more a virtue. As conservative institutions, moreover, established churches have everywhere tended to become allied with the monarch or ruling class, to sanctify the social *status quo,* and to suppress the revolutionary implications in the teaching of the founders. For all such reasons organized religion in advanced societies has almost always lagged behind intellectual development and social change. No great church has ever led the struggle for either freedom of thought or political freedom.

Similarly established churches alter the service of God, beginning with their characteristic stress on ritual. Their God is likely to be not so much in freedom as in necessity, ordinarily declaring that man's primary duty is to serve him, and dictating his menial duties. "It is pathetic," Santayana remarked, "to observe how lowly are the motives that religion, even the highest, attributes to the deity, and from what a hard-pressed and bitter existence they have been drawn. To be given the best morsel, to be remembered, to be praised, to be obeyed blindly and punctiliously—these have been thought points of honor with the gods, for which they would dispense favors and punishments on the most exorbitant scale." Everywhere some gods became gods of love, but the supreme god remained a god of power, to be feared as well as loved. If the fear of God may be salutary, or what men most need, it still does not make for freedom. While primitives may be bedeviled, they are rarely so humbled as worshipers of the Almighty have been by warnings against pride in man's own achievements.

Christianity in particular became a positive enemy to freedom because of its exclusiveness, an inheritance from Judaism that passed into Mohammedanism as well. Its God had announced himself as a jealous God, who commanded first of all that men not only believe in him but reject the gods of all other peoples as false gods. To this family of religions is due a major innovation in man's history—religious fanaticism. When Christianity won political power its authoritarian church denied freedom to men of other faiths. It began a systematic persecution of pagans, Jews, and then heretics; not only belief in God but correct opinions about his nature became a prerequisite for citizenship or any human rights. Christendom went on to make by far the bloodiest record of persecution in religious history—what the devout Lord Acton himself described as "the appalling edifice of intolerance, tyranny, cruelty, which believers in Christ built up, to perpetuate their belief." The rise of Protestantism and the consequent holy wars between Protestants and Catholics eventuated in a struggle for religious freedom, or freedom of conscience, which then promoted the cause of civil liberties; but the victory of this cause may be ascribed to a tragic failure of Christianity. In France and America freethinkers played the most prominent part in the struggle for freedom. For Christianity had long represented the major opposition to freedom of thought; and even today "freethinker" has unsavory connotations for ordinary Christians.

There remains popular religion, the thought and feeling of the masses of simple worshipers under all the higher religions. Here are to be found the most primitive, universal, enduring elements of religion. They include ritual and prayer, to propitiate the deity and secure special favors; the worship of images, relics, saints, and sacred cows; heavens and hells with angels and demons, sensual joys and torments: altogether a miscellany of prehistoric superstitions, alike reflecting pathetic hopes and fears. As the Grand Inquisitor said, what the great majority of men seek is not God but the miraculous. With this they usually need a Devil—another possibly salutary figure, but unfortunately apt to turn into a foreigner, a Jew, a scapegoat. Whatever the name of its deities, popular religion has always had an inescapably vulgar, materialistic aspect, which today is dressed up as "the power of positive thinking." Its indignities are not simply humiliating in view of the hard lot most men have had to bear throughout history, with little earthly help from their churches. It should nevertheless be kept in mind, since churchmen are given to equating religion with spirituality. As for freedom, it may relieve anxiety and so help men to achieve other purposes, realize other capacities; but such freedom has ordinarily been a by-product of organized religion, not its avowed end. Historically there has been no clear parallel between the growth of freedom and the development of religion, including Christianity, if only because freedom has simply never been a major concern of religion until recent centuries in the West.

Other positive contributions of *historic* religion may accordingly be viewed with some irony. In their worldly success, established churches stimulated creativity in fields of worldly endeavor to which their founders were more or less indifferent. They helped to give birth to new civilizations, as well as new empires. They harbored the glories of religious art—glories denounced by some saints as corruptions of the true faith, or sinful ostentation. They produced theology, which perhaps did more to confuse than to clarify the true faith, yet encouraged inquiry and the growth of learning. Medieval theology transmitted to modern science the basic assumption of an intelligible, lawful world, which men proceeded to master for their own purposes. Christianity has been especially productive of worldly works because of its militancy and its deep tensions. Preaching a timeless kingdom not of this world, it was nonetheless unlike Hinduism and Buddhism in that it insisted on the reality and the importance of this world—one in which God himself had appeared, in historical time, in order to redeem it by his suffering. Soldiers of the Cross were given to an overweening pride and self-righteousness, but by the same token to an extraordinary creative energy.

And sometimes to charity too. For in spite of all their shortcomings—in part because of their shortcomings—established churches have also kept alive the idealism of their founders, fitting it to the capacities of ordinary men and the uses of everyday life. They have produced many earnest pastors who were better shepherds because they were neither theologians nor saints. Hence popular religion has not been sheer superstition. Simple worshipers have often given proof of a simple piety, in dealings with fellow men as well as with deity. In their lowliness, they might best exemplify the virtues of faith, hope, and charity.

Today the much-abused Christian spirit may have more meaning and force than appears on the surface, or in the vulgar travesties of religious revivals. The impossibility of measuring its influence, the often flagrant inconsistency between belief and behavior (which can be roughly measured in public opinion polls), the much more obvious influence of material interests, the awareness that most popular belief is mostly rationalization, the common American belief that any belief will do so long as it is "sincere"—for such reasons we may drastically discount the power of Christian faith. Nevertheless liberals and pragmatists who do not subscribe to this faith perhaps bank on it more than they realize. They assume a spirit of good will when they contend for the rights of common men or propose the method of intelligence. They may forget that the very abuse of the Christian spirit—all the cant in a nation that passes a law declaring itself "under God," as if it could be under anything else—indicates that the ideal is still alive; for the cant gets its force from the ideal, just as dishonesty may pay only because most men are honest most of the time.

All in all, religion can help to conserve the principles of freedom in a society dedicated to such principles. It may be an indispensable support, if only because most men would still feel lost without it. Yet its primary concern is still with other ends. It can thrive under almost any kind of state, as throughout history it has supported every kind, and it might thrive more on the loss of freedom, especially the loss of faith in man's powers, as early Christianity did. It still works both to inspire and to constrain, to enlighten and to obscure, to unite and to divide, to free and to enslave the spirit, to hearten and to discourage earthly purposes. A student of freedom must therefore try to make out the dominant tendencies of a given religion, in a given society, at a given time. In our own society he must reckon with liberal Christianity, which has come to accept the ideal of freedom of conscience and so to belie the provincial assumption, based on Judaeo-Christian history, that the religious spirit is by its nature intolerant; while he must also reckon with the powers of orthodoxy and neofundamentalism, the persistent tendencies to self-righteousness, and the fashionable tendencies to deplore a faith in man. But whatever his own faith, he needs to distinguish the cause of religion from the cause of freedom.

IX.

Art

A GREAT artist, wrote André Gide, is necessarily a non-conformist. Since the Romantic Movement the artist has commonly been regarded as a born individualist, always likely to be a rebel against his society. In the popular mind he is naturally different from solid citizens, more or less eccentric. To sophisticates his difference is his badge of distinction, if also the key to his natural fate of maladjustment. Psychoanalysts study him as a dreamer or escapist. He may fancy himself as a Bohemian, an "outsider," an exile from Philistia, an avant-gardiste, or now a last-ditch defender of culture. In any case he looks like an apostle of freedom, instinctively hostile to all convention and constraint. It would appear that freedom is essential to creativity, even synonymous with it, and that only in freedom can genius realize itself.

But it does not so appear to a historian. On the record, art has served all kinds of causes. Perhaps the least common before our time has been the cause of artistic independence, or any declared right to self-expression. Typically art has conformed to the ruling interests of a society, expressed its accepted ideals. The rebel has been a rare type. The golden ages have not been uniformly ages of intellectual freedom, much less civil and political freedom. Great art has been produced under diverse conditions, commonly including despotism.

Most conspicuously, indeed, art has been a conservative force. At the dawn of civilization it served immediately the interests of high priests and kings. If monumental architecture and its sculptured accessories were not consciously designed to awe the multitude, they at least had the effect of keeping it submissive, widening the gulf between the god-king and the commoner. Thereafter art remained the servant of the ruling class. Humble artisans did humble work for the common folk; major works were commissioned by the privileged few, to the greater glory of their gods or of themselves. While great artists came out of the folk, few expressed folk interests and fewer proclaimed anything like folk rights. Literature necessarily became the possession of an elite, since the masses were illiterate, and it naturally confirmed aristocratic values. To be "fine art," it had to keep remote from the common life. Classics everywhere have been literally classy. The magic of the written word—most apparent in "scriptures" or "bibles"—also impeded freedom of thought by sanctifying the reigning superstitions, immortalizing delusion.

The historic alliance of fine art and privilege strengthened the tendency of art to become set in its ways. As a lover of form, the artist is apt to welcome convention; generally he has worked contentedly in styles developed by earlier masters. Privileged classes have been as prone to traditionalism, perhaps welcoming superficial novelty, but seldom encouraging

radical departure from aristocratic canons. The new styles
that did develop, as old styles became exhausted or societies
changed in spite of themselves, were not heralded by mani-
festoes of intellectual or artistic freedom.

Nevertheless there are deep and abiding connections between art and freedom, broadly conceived. Rooted in man's
natural pleasure in the forms and rhythms about him and
within him, art is a fulfillment of his impulse to explore and
discover, realize the exciting potentialities of the natural world
—an impulse most apparent in the unschooled child. It has
insistently declared a lust for life in this world, which the spiritual leaders of man have often branded as transitory, illusory,
or evil. Thus the exuberance of Hindu art belied the negations
of Hindu religion; worshipers of Buddha heralded the extinc-
tion of all passion and desire by erecting gorgeous temples and
statues of fat, smiling Buddhas; the mystical poets of Islam
reveled in erotic imagery; and Gothic artists carved scenes of
tipplers and brawlers on stalls from which worshipers raised
their thoughts to heaven, or to gargoyles.

Deeper connections with freedom may be obscured by the
romantic notion of art as self-expression, fancy-free. For the
secret of great art is not free fancy, which is all too common.
It is mastery: mastery of materials, of medium, of experience.
For this reason it is a major means to self-realization, as well
as a major end. The artist may appear to copy the external
world in naturalistic art, or directly to express the inner world
of feeling in expressionistic or non-representational art, but in
either case his work is literally an ideal creation, stamped by

his own spirit, bent to his own purposes. It is a primary means of transforming nature into culture, building and furnishing a world of man's own. In this broad sense all art may be considered essentially humanistic, or in Thomas Mann's ideal terms, "the free service of humanity." As such, it reflects all the vagaries, ambiguities, and follies of the human spirit. It may ennoble man or debase him, enhance life or degrade it, emancipate the spirit or enslave it. It may provide an escape from triviality into an ideal realm, or an escape from responsibility into a dream world. The world it creates may be serene, radiant, or grand; fearful, dark, or grotesque. But its ultimate effect has been to heighten man's consciousness of both nature and human nature, of his own powers of heart and mind, and so, perhaps, of finer, fuller possibilities of life.

Art grown self-conscious may therefore contribute more directly to the growth of freedom. In Homer's Greece it signaled the triumph of man over destiny—over the fatality he could face and master through his art; the gods themselves were then drawn into the service of conscious ideals of freedom and culture, most notably in democratic Athens. In Renaissance Europe, especially republican Florence, art again both expressed and inspired a new faith in man's powers, new hopes for a richer life on earth. Many Western artists have in fact been conscious apostles of freedom, rebels against traditional authority. The liberal tradition that grew out of the humanistic faith has enlisted such diverse writers as Rabelais, Montaigne, Erasmus, Milton, Voltaire, Schiller, Shelley, Pushkin, Whitman, and Mann. And once a society has come to know intellectual and political freedom, this may well be a vital factor in its art. The decline of art that accompanied the decline of freedom in the last centuries of the Roman Empire may portend the fate of art in totalitarian countries today.

As usual, then, we need to be wary of generalizations about the role of art in the abstract, need to look first to a given art in a given society. The culture as a whole affects its role. But here too we need to be wary of stock generalizations. Art is always a partial reflection of a society, or more precisely a refraction. It is likely to give misleading impressions, because it seldom gives an adequate idea of the common life. It may or may not flourish on the growing edge of a society, anticipate new ideals or the actual future in store. It may provide the most comprehensive expression of the aspirations of an age, as in Dante's *Divine Comedy,* or it may fail to express the most vital movements of its age, as in the early centuries of Christianity. It is not a reliable index to social health, energy, or creativity. The golden ages of art do not clearly mark the zenith of a society, often preceding the highest developments in not only material wealth and power but philosophy and science, civility and sophistication, ethical and religious idealism. (Even Arnold Toynbee gave up the effort to find a "law" in the arts corresponding to his law that material and spiritual achievement are antithetical.) Neither does a decline in art necessarily signify decadence in the society as a whole. Strictly, we cannot even speak of "art" in this way. Architecture, sculpture, painting, music, and literature do not uniformly flourish and decline together, fit into common patterns.

In short, art is not merely a product of its age or a reflection of the historical process. It is to some extent an autonomous activity, ruled by its own potentialities and necessities. And it is always the creation of individual artists. The greater artists express some personal vision even when they are working within a fixed convention and are not consciously aspiring to originality. In ages of disorder, and especially in free societies, they may speak more plainly for themselves, express the whole range of attitudes from acceptance to rejection of the ruling interests and traditional values. Such individuality would seem unmistakable, but it is often obscured by a kind of unconscious, innocent determinism of modern historical scholars, eager to track down sources, to ferret out influences, to chart tendencies, and to pin the art-work down to "the age." If few artists outside the Western world have been avowed rebels or crusaders, many have exhibited an originality or independence that manifests the actual freedom of the human spirit, and that might weaken the despotism of custom and conventional belief.

All this implies that art is a positive factor in history, molding as well as expressing the mentality of its age. In our own practical, positivistic age men are inclined to assume that it has no influence worth mentioning, especially because they consider it at most an elegant pastime, not a significant way of knowing and dealing with "reality." Historians are likely to emphasize the more obvious influence of society on art. Yet a student of freedom can scarcely disregard a mode of creativity that has been so prominent in most of the great creative ages, and so often on the forefront of growing civilizations. If it was more an effect than a cause of the growth, art was at least a spur, and in the forms of epic, scripture, and monumental architecture both shaped and vitalized national and religious ideals. Given the immense amount of time, effort, and wealth that all previous societies have lavished on it, it plainly does satisfy some deep need and therefore presumably does have some significant effect on men. Rulers have always recognized its obvious effects in stirring emotion, molding sentiment and desire. Tacitly they have appeared to agree with Oscar Wilde that life imitates art more than art imitates life. And with the invention of the printing press, literature in particular has unquestionably become a powerful factor. It created a major issue of freedom—freedom of the press—as monarchs and churchmen soon honored it by trying to keep it censored.

Today practical men are also the chief witnesses to the power of art. Dictators not only keep literature under control but have shown concern over the orthodoxy of painting and music. Advertisers exploit the resources of photography, painting, music, and poetry to sell their wares. Big industries make millions manufacturing popular art, molding life to the vulgar heart's desire. Lovers of art may exaggerate the good it does, or assume too easily that fine art has only good effects, but its power over the minds of men has never been more apparent than in this age of mass media, whose leaders proclaim that the real business of life is business. No well-wisher of democracy can afford to ignore the issues of democratic culture. One might therefore shudder as he recalls the old saying: Let me write the songs of a people and I care not who writes its laws. "God Bless America!"—or God help it.

X.

Philosophy

FORMAL philosophy in the Western world got under way, appropriately, with the simple statement of Thales of Miletus: "All things are made of water." In view of the manifold appearances of the world and the universal, timeless habit of explaining them in mythical terms, this statement was an astonishingly bold, brilliant speculation; and it was erroneous. It signaled the birth of conscious theory, the effort to explain the world by pure reason—the emancipation of mind from the delusions of magic and miracle that Renan hailed as the only miracle in history. It opened up a whole new realm of experience because it was an emancipation as well from purely practical thought, the immediate necessities that magic had served. Instead of merely stumbling over problems, man was now deliberately creating new problems. And he has been thinking them up ever since. By now we all know the costs of this miracle, in basic uncertainty and perplexity, permanent confusion over first and last principles. From the beginning the emancipated mind displayed inclinations to create more ambitious forms of delusion, more systematic means of tyrannizing over thought. Freed from the constraints of practice, while still ignorant of the nature of mind, philosophy would assert the omnipotence of pure reason.

Typically its disciples have shown a preference for theories that discredit the world of immediate experience in which ordinary men enjoy their freedom. Like Thales, most philosophers have sought the One—the essential reality, the ultimate cause—and depreciated the many as "mere" appearances. Similarly they have considered permanence a much more distinguished kind of reality than change or growth, looked for a principle of immutable Being instead of possible Becoming; in social and political life they have conceived the ideal as stability, not growth. Their abiding passion for cosmic law and order at any cost has often made them blind or hostile to the rich possibilities inherent in copiousness, variety, spontaneity, and uncertainty. Philosophical idealists, who have made the most exalted claims for the human spirit, have had the strongest bent to restrict its actual freedom, in the interest of "true freedom," the service of their cosmic spiritual reality, or in a lofty unconcern about the temporal conditions of life in the degraded natural world, the only world surely known to man. In all schools thinkers have aspired to finality, and therefore tended to confine thought in closed systems. One might say that philosophy has thrived in spite of itself, or on its limitations and failures—or the endless disagreements among its practitioners, who can never prove the absolute, eternal truths that most have asserted, and that many still assert are the only kind of truth that can really do for man.

Yet philosophy has made its own provision for these occupational hazards, by its essential rationalism. It must appeal to reason in order to demonstrate its claims, even when these are claims to an intuitive, mystical knowledge beyond reason. It has continuously undermined its pretensions to finality, not only because philosophers can always be trusted to disagree, but because its demonstrations are always open to logical criticism, as myth and magic are not on their own ground. If theory has often declared its independence of practice or ordinary experience, it cannot wander wherever it listeth, and sooner or later is subjected to empirical test. In emancipating the mind, philosophy also disciplined it.

As it has worked to keep the mind active, so in the long run philosophy has tended to keep thought free. It breaks up the cake of custom, which alone can give the certainty and stability it has aspired to. The new problems it creates, the questions it raises with every Q.E.D., are new possibilities, offering more alternatives for choice. Speculative, critical thought may produce theories hostile to freedom, but without such thought no society can realize and maintain a conscious ideal of freedom. It is no accident that philosophy has been most vigorous, varied, and restless in the Western world.

Even so it brings up the inevitable question: How much difference has philosophy actually made in the course of history? It is repeatedly said that Plato, for instance, has been the most influential philosopher in Western tradition, and it seems clear that he has had considerable influence—on other philosophers. But has he had any to speak of on social and political life? Did he have anything to do with the growth of

Western civilization, or the great changes that have come over it?

In the past thinkers were doubtless wont to exaggerate their importance, out of professional pride. Today there is little such danger. Aside from deterministic theories that explicitly deny the independent power of philosophy, we have grown much more aware of material factors, economic interests, unconscious tendencies, irrational drives—all the unideal forces behind ideas, which give them their force, and which plainly influence philosophers, giving a naïve air to their traditional claim of speaking as oracles of pure reason. Hence Platonic idealism may look like a mere reflection of the failure of Athens in the Peloponnesian War, a refuge from the real world in which history was being made. Of more empirical, seemingly influential thought, such as the political philosophy of John Locke, it may be said that Locke merely justified the English Revolution that was already under way, and that Americans in turn used his thought to justify a revolution they were going to make anyway. Like all collective action, this revolution was a confused affair, largely unplanned, with one thing leading to another and men trying to keep up with the event. It recalls us to the world of practical affairs, where philosophy is discounted most rudely and thoroughly. The hardheaded businessman knows that "mere theory" gets us nowhere.

Still, this man is himself always operating on theories. Upon demand, he can produce a patchwork of vague, incoherent theories that he calls his philosophy of life. Probably they include the Platonic theory that he has an immortal soul. With it is bundled a crude kind of materialism; the dualism harks back to Descartes. In business he has been devoted to the more novel theory of *laissez faire,* formulated by Adam Smith and promulgated by thinkers who in their time were not conservatives. He gets angry about the "socialistic" theories that may be traced to Karl Marx, and that nevertheless even many Republicans have somehow come to accept. His baffled anger suggests that his hardheaded distrust of intellectuals may be unfortunate, since he is quite unequipped to do any hard thinking himself about the nature of man, society, or state, or to understand the revolutionary world in which he lives. At the same time his fear of "visionary idealists" implies a belief that they can do real harm, and so may not be such ineffectual fellows after all. As an American, he may even applaud the visionary idealism incorporated in the theory on which this nation was founded—more consciously and deliberately than any great nation before it.

In view of such typical confusion, we cannot hope to disentangle all the stands in Western tradition, isolate the consequences of any one theory, measure the force of any one thinker. Plato is a clear example of the difficulties. While he was no champion of freedom, for reasons historically understandable, his own thought was remarkable for its freedom, its range, mobility, and suggestiveness. Unmistakably a product of Greek culture, it was still highly individualized. It had little apparent influence on his own age, which was moving away from him. It had much more on later ages, especially when it entered Christianity, to embark on a long career in a much greater world than he knew or dreamed of. Plato would surely have been surprised, probably dismayed, by what many later philosophers, mystics, and poets made of Platonism; but this was further proof of the fertility and vitality of his thought. His influence was pervasive, largely indirect, to my knowledge never so decisive as that, say, of Newton or Marx. It has probably been exaggerated because he became the symbolic father of philosophical idealism. The contribution of any one thinker is always likely to be exaggerated when he becomes the symbol of a tradition or a new movement.

Nevertheless the tradition remains a vital factor, the movement may be decisive. Americans very possibly might have written their Declaration of Independence had John Locke never lived, but they could not have done so without the work of all the men who contributed to the Age of the Enlightenment. The Declaration could never have been made in the ancient East, or made good in the Middle Ages. For such reasons, too, a history of ideas will differ from a history of formal philosophy. The greatness or the originality of a thinker is not necessarily an index to his historical influence, still less to his contribution to the cause of freedom. It may obscure the contributions of lesser thinkers, as Aristotle's defense of the institution of slavery has obscured the plain implication that other Greeks were attacking it. These Greeks prepared the way for the Stoic idea of natural law, which came down through the unoriginal Cicero, entered Roman law, and had a much more marked influence on Western political tradition than has

Plato's *Republic*. As a herald of a new era, Locke similarly seems more important than the more profound, logical Spinoza. And no philosopher has had such wide influence as the founders of the higher religions, among whom the prophets of Israel, Jesus, and Mohammed were as innocent of formal theology as of metaphysics or epistemology.

Yet their influence also belies a purely materialistic interpretation of history. In a comprehensive view it appears that the most decisive ideas in history have been abstract ideas and visionary ideals. Out of these grew not only the higher religions but science and democracy, and more lately Communism. And philosophy has been so intimately connected with the growth and spread of such ideas and ideals that the burden of proof lies with those who would deny it significant influence on history.

One who does not deny it still has to reckon with the strictly incalculable—he keeps running up against Platos. The determinist, the system-builder, the lawmaker—all the philosophical dictators of history have an easier time of it, and at that may win a reputation for profundity. But they too, and above all the Marxists, are products of a philosophical tradition that most clearly illustrates the practical importance of theory. For the Greeks, with whom the conscious faith in the power of mind entered history, the main uses of mind were more to contemplate, speculate, or explain than to transform or re-create. In Western civilization abstract ideas have been systemically put to work, translated into programs to conquer nature and make over state and society. Ideals of social justice going back to the prophets of Israel were likewise translated into programs of action. Indignant as the prophets were over the oppression of the poor, they had accomplished little if anything on their behalf, because they never proposed any concrete measures of reform or made any effort to change the social and political system of Israel; and no more had Christian saints. The English Utilitarians, led by the unsaintly philosopher Jeremy Bentham, did much more for the poor of England by working for positive legal reforms. The West developed the unique type of the professional reformer, corresponding to the professional innovator in science and technology.

XI.

Science

ALTHOUGH all civilized societies have had considerable empirical knowledge, or the rudiments of science, science as we know it is only a few centuries old. It is now not merely a body of knowledge but a systematic method of getting more knowledge, which has made possible a steady advance unparalleled in any society before our own. Unlike religion and art, accordingly, it has not been a continuous factor in the history of freedom. Yet it must be considered immediately in any study of freedom. It has profoundly influenced both the methods and the premises of all inquiry, transforming our basic conceptions of the nature of the universe, of man, and of his history on earth. We may affect to despise science and all its works, but we cannot escape its influence, cannot think as if it had not been. To know ourselves, we have to be aware of what it has done for us and to us.

Its most obvious effect, of course, has been an enormous increase in man's knowledge and his power over nature, the range of his effective freedom. It is the clearest demonstration of the actual power of intelligence, more especially of the emancipated mind. Hence it had much to do with the growth of intellectual and political freedom. *Nullius in verba* ran the motto the Royal Society was founded on in the seventeenth century—"we accept no authority"; as science triumphed over the opposition of the most ancient, revered authorities, men drew the evident conclusion—thought must be kept free. They went on to a rational criticism of social institutions, such as absolute monarchy, that were based on authority. They seized upon the democratic implications of the scientific method: a public method open to all men by virtue of their common possession of reason, not requiring noble birth, priestly initiation, or divine guidance, and resulting in a democratic conception of the universe as an open book. By "the light of science," in the words of Thomas Jefferson, men were led to the basic faith of the Age of the Enlightenment—in reason, in freedom, in progress—which became the ruling faith of Western democracy.

As familiar today, however, are the paradoxical results of the triumph of science, even apart from the frightful uses that men have made of the power got by it. Its triumph was due immediately to an efficient concentration on the quantitative, mechanistic aspects of the external world; and its disciples then forgot that they were abstracting, mistook their partial description for the essential or the only truth about this world. The qualities of experience that they left out, the felt values, the whole inner world of consciousness—such primary meanings were discredited as secondary, merely subjective, or at best of a lower grade of reality. In achieving autonomy for their special purposes, scientific thinkers in effect denied the autonomy of man. When they turned their attention to man, many regarded him too as a machine. Trying to explain him by the same concepts that physicists had used so successfully, they shied away from such indispensable concepts as purpose and value. In general, man was belittled and his world dehumanized. Even the immense expansion of knowledge brought about by science has narrowed the consciousness of many men by forcing an intensive specialization, keeping them in grooves.

More paradoxically, this most triumphant demonstration of the power of human reason has helped to undermine the faith in reason, inspiring a radical skepticism about both its theoretical and its practical uses. The universe that once seemed an open book has grown steadily queerer and more mysterious, until it now seems more unintelligible than it ever has in the history of thought. The Principle of Indeterminacy sets definite limits to what we can know about electrons. Social scientists have set as sharp limits to our power of rational judgment in matters of values, reducing these to mere custom. Positivists have labeled "meaningless" statements about the good life as well as God; and although some are beginning to find room for ethical judgments, they still insist that these are not "cognitive," effectively divorcing values and knowledge. Reason, it would appear, can give us no truth in these vital matters—it can only tell us not to ask the most significant questions. Meanwhile its power of control in human affairs has been seriously questioned, when not denied outright by scientific determinists. Psychologists and sociologists have emphasized the extent of reflex or conditioned behavior, the power of unconscious or irrational drives. Semi- and pseudo-scientists have directly assaulted human dignity by "motivational research" put at the disposal of advertisers, specialists in exploiting the irrational.

Yet such paradoxes should not blind us to the obvious. Science is in fact a triumph of human reason, and its rise a landmark in the history of human freedom. It at once emancipated the mind more fully and disciplined it more strictly than had philosophy. It remains man's surest method of discovery, and so of further development. It has given us our most positive, reliable knowledge about the natural world, knowledge no less usable because of uncertainties about its theoretical foundations; as the universe got more mysterious, scientists got hold of atomic power. Twentieth-century physics is one of the most extraordinarily imaginative, daring, exhilarating adventures in the history of human thought. It is a supreme demonstration of the real freedom and power of thought.

By scientific methods we have likewise amassed a great deal of positive knowledge about the nature and history of man. If this knowledge does not yield conclusive answers to questions about purpose and value, the uses of freedom, it cannot be ignored in any intelligent consideration of these questions. With it we have a great deal of suggestive, illuminating theory in psychology and the social sciences, theory that we may use more profitably if we keep in mind that these are not exact sciences comparable to physics; their practitioners tend to make extravagant claims simply because their scientific status is questionable. For all such excesses the scientific community itself provides a corrective by its aboveboard methods, in its quest of a public kind of truth, disciplined by a constant insistence on correspondence to the facts and a continued refusal to accept on authority. Science has its orthodoxy, but it is the one orthodoxy to welcome innovation and dissent, to provide systematic means for criticism and self-correction, and always to insist on the absolute necessity of independent thought.

Hence the skepticism inspired by science has grown out of a positive faith, which may illumine the principle of freedom of thought that the rise of science helped to establish. One traditional argument for this principle has been based on such skepticism. In contending against ancient authorities, men declared that no authority possessed ultimate certainty, and that religious differences in particular should be tolerated because it is impossible to demonstrate which religion is true. As Mill wrote in *On Liberty,* no man and no society had a right to claim infallibility. The same argument is behind the democratic sentiment that every man has a right to his own opinion. And it points to a revolutionary value of the scientific spirit, which represents a victory over the age-old habit of passionately claiming certitude in matters not in fact certainly known.

Nevertheless skepticism alone is not a sufficient defense of freedom of thought. If it is all merely a matter of opinion, it would be reasonable enough for Church and State to suppress all heretical, subversive opinion; there is no cause of truth to suffer. Liberals would have no firm ground on which to condemn intolerance, bigotry, prejudice—the most common kinds of opinion. Science constitutes a more positive argument for freedom of thought, on grounds of respect for knowledge and love of truth. It claims the authority of positive knowledge, and a positive means to more knowledge; its pioneers spoke with this authority when they rejected traditional authorities. It is a declaration that a man does *not* have a right to any opinion—only to reasoned opinions, based on the best available knowledge. It is a moral as well as intellectual commitment, to fidelity to truth and truthfulness. Because so many of its followers have shied away from the ideas of purpose and value, we may forget that science itself is an intensely purposeful activity, and is based on a faith in the value of truth and the spirit that seeks truth.

The scientist accordingly does not claim freedom in research merely as a private right, or a means of expressing his individuality. He claims it as a member of a community that exemplifies a truly rational freedom: a freedom to seek truth and to follow wherever the quest may lead, but a freedom always controlled by respect for one's fellow seekers, by the requirement of disinterestedness, and by the severe discipline of scientific methods. Unlike business, political, and religious communities, the scientific community maintains its ideals without parade and without coercion. The individual scientist may of course be inordinately fond of his own theory, his brain child; he is neither an intellectual saint nor an impersonal monster. His community may nevertheless be called an ideal intellectual commonwealth: co-operative in essence, free in membership, democratic in procedure, impersonal in standards, international in scope.

Its universality still needs to be stressed. Defenders of traditional metaphysical or religious interests often describe science as only another philosophy or sect, even a form of Western provincialism, to be contrasted, say, with the mysticism of the East. It does indeed involve philosophical presuppositions, necessarily operating on naturalistic premises, in its own realm rejecting the authority of supernatural revelation. Yet science has been welcomed by all the countries of the non-Western world, as Christianity has not been and no philosophical or religious sect is ever likely to be. It is a method for attaining an objective kind of truth acceptable to all men, not relative to a particular culture or tied to a particular philosophy. It is the best available means for rising above all political, national, racial, and religious differences, getting free from sectarian prejudices. It is the one international language.

By now only the naïve can dream that in time science will answer all questions, settle all differences, or that man will ever be able to manage his life in a purely scientific spirit, by scientific methods. The limits of scientific knowledge are the more necessary to keep in mind as one proposes to follow the lead of science as far as it can take him. There remain the uncertainties in the high matters of the good life, the ends of freedom, and beyond these the metaphysical and religious possibilities that to many men are all-important. We may therefore understand the pleasure with which some religious thinkers have seized on the Principle of Indeterminacy. But we need not accept their strange conclusion that science is somehow discredited by its acknowledgments of limits and uncertainties, and that their own arbitrary claims to certainty are thereby strengthened. There is no good substitute for reliable knowledge, no good reason to rejoice in ignorance. The scientific spirit, grown out of the disinterested pursuit of truth that began with Thales in Greece, entails a humble respect both for fact and for mystery that has brought to some men a kind of "spiritual freedom." In any case it remains our surest means to freedom in thought.

XII.

The Idea of History

ALTHOUGH the ancient Greeks were the first people to make history a subject of rational inquiry, all civilized peoples have had myths, legends, and annals that constituted something like a theory of history. They had some idea of their past, and with it notions about where the human race came from and why. With it they also had some image of their possible or probable future, and usually some notions about where the race is going. However vague, incoherent, or unconscious, such ideas are an important factor in the actual history that men keep making. And especially important for the student of freedom is their image of the future. If all societies have kept working and hoping for something or other, as men must and do to go on living, their beliefs have differed widely in how open they left the future, and to what kinds of possibilities.

Some peoples, notably the ancient Egyptians, believed that their society was essentially static and immutable. The Egyptians were therefore disposed to feel confident of their future in good times, and hopeless in bad times, but they could hardly conceive of any essential change or basic reform, anything they could do except maintain or restore the old order. Other peoples, as in ancient Mesopotamia, felt that the future was open but only to uncertainty, very possibly to disaster; they looked forward in anxiety more than hope, to a future that man might determine by the arts of divination, but not by rational effort of his own. Everywhere men dreamed of a better state, but typically they located it in the past—in a Garden of Eden, a Golden Age—or in a heavenly afterlife. The more thoughtful believed that time was the enemy of man and his works, so their main hope was to arrest change; they did not welcome change or bank on it. The most thoughtful conceived change as endless recurrence, history as endless cycle. On earth, in effect, the human race was going nowhere —only round and round, up and down, over and over again, to no apparent purpose. When a society seemed to be in the downswing (and their society seemed so to almost all thinkers who conceived history as cycle), there was nothing men could do about it except resign themselves.

The conspicuous example of how much practical difference the image of the future may make is the novel, revolutionary Western idea of progress. Although past societies might feel complacent in the belief that they were sitting on top of the world, none dreamed that man by his own efforts could indefinitely improve his life on earth. The unique faith that the future would be ever better than the past rose with modern science. It was intimately connected with the growth of freedom, the emancipation from ancient authorities. It helps to explain why modern civilization has been by all odds the most dynamic in history. For the faith in progress begot not only a hopeful spirit but a *will* to progress. Assuring men that they do have the power to choose and carry out their own purposes, it stimulated them to develop their powers and to raise their sights. The seemingly odd devotion to posterity that it inspired —"O posterity, holy and sacred!" Diderot exclaimed—may seem less odd when we recall the millions of immigrants in America who toiled in the hope that their children would enjoy better opportunities, through education, than they themselves had.

The dynamism of the idea of progress has naturally been most apparent in America. The past was no model for Americans in their "new land," a land of opportunity. As they prospered they set about removing the ancient barriers of poverty and ignorance, extending the opportunities of common men, enlisting the energies of all. Whereas men in other societies had typically sought wisdom or "freedom" by reducing desire, even trying to eliminate it, Americans kept multiplying their desires. They have always been buoyed up by the axiomatic assumption that America was going somewhere, had a great future. In times of trouble they have never been resigned, but have taken for granted that something should and could be done about the trouble. Always suspicious of government, inclined to believe that every new action by it is a threat to their freedom, they automatically still raise the cry: Why doesn't the government do something about it?

The idea of progress also helped to inspire the study of history, as a means of advancing the cause of progress. Thus

Voltaire exposed the tyranny of priests and kings that had blighted most of the past; Gibbon warned of the dangers of barbarism and Christianity, which had triumphed over the great Roman Empire. In the last century Lord Acton was most earnest and explicit about the high mission of history, which was to emancipate man from the tyranny of the past, the perennial enemy of freedom. In this century Bury had much the same faith as he wrote the history of the idea of progress, and the history of freedom of thought. Most historians at least believe that a knowledge of the past is of some use as a warning and a guide, a means to keeping the future open to better possibilities.

Now I have already noted that the popular faith in progress —a complacent faith in an automatic, purely material progress—has been a threat as well as a stimulus to hopes of a better future. In America it has encouraged social irresponsibility, confirmed the popular resentment of critics as spoilsports, swollen the popular hysteria over revolutionaries. In the Communist world the "iron laws" that guarantee progress to the utopian classless society have justified violence and tyranny, iron methods of disposing of perverse people who get in the way of this progress. The intensive professional study of history has likewise brought in the usual train of ambiguities. It produced many national histories that reduced the image of man's future to the manifest destiny of the nation, fostered the tribalism that intensified conflict between nations. It led to the kind of historicism that sees in the past only the working of necessity, whether mechanical or dialectical, and so in effect substitutes history for judgment, declares that whatever was and is, is right. Of late it has engendered considerable scorn of the idea of progress. Some eminent historians are looking back to religion as the only hope for the future, or as a means of escape from the future.[1]

Needless to add, the Western faith in progress has been badly shaken by recent history. This suggests that a society's image of the future is less a cause than a symptom or by-product of its basic mentality. As such, it is no less significant to a student of freedom; it helps to define this mentality, to detect changes in it, to disclose the growth or the loss of confidence in man's powers. But it may also have a positive influence on behavior, as does the fever that is the symptom of disease. It reinforces the ruling attitudes or gives more impetus to changing attitudes; it intensifies the common hopes and fears that strengthen or weaken resolution and responsibility. The growing doubts about progress may lessen the chances of a better future. One may venture the prophecy that if men in the Western democracies ever lose their distinctive hope of progress, they are pretty sure to lose their basic freedoms too—or, more precisely, will already have lost them.

In spite of this possibility, one may also venture the assertion that the heartening idea of progress is to some extent a valid one. Granted all the costs and the uncertainties, there

---

[1] In his influential *Christianity and History*, for example, Herbert Butterfield assured Christians that they had no reason for anguish over their earthly prospects or the possible loss of their freedom because they would always have Christ. "Hold to Christ," he concluded, "and for the rest be totally uncommitted."

has unquestionably been a material progress, which one may appreciate by contemplating the appalling poverty, disease, and wretchedness of the masses in most of the non-Western world. As unquestionable is the intellectual progress, the essential condition of all the distinctive values of civilization, including the "spiritual" values; religious thinkers who attack the idea of progress as sinful pride forget that they do so in the name of Christianity, a "higher" religion. To Western man the growth of freedom has represented another major advance. The evils and follies that cause many to despair of our civilization seem more dreadful because of the higher expectations we have developed, the higher standards by which we judge—in particular the standards of "human rights," largely unrecognized in the past.

This is also to say that the idea of progress still pervades the Western world, is still at least a live hope. The flood of urgent books about our crisis—modern man at the crossroads, and the choice he must make—is another significant symptom, immediately somewhat depressing, but in a historical perspective heartening. There was no such flood of treatises in the declining Roman Empire, or in any other dying civilization. Energetic rulers or ambitious would-be rulers kept striving; thinkers and writers generally looked back nostalgically to the good old days, or looked forward only to the hereafter, and meanwhile counseled the wisdom of resignation that for the masses had always been the only available wisdom. Most Westerners apparently still feel that we can do something about our crisis, have some choice in futures. They keep busy on such extraordinary projects as rockets to the moon—an idea that only a few centuries ago would have seemed as perfectly fantastic as a cow jumping over the moon. If we manage to avoid catastrophe, men may look back upon our age as one of the greatest in all history; or if they do not, the reason may be that the will to progress will have led them to achievements as far beyond our ken as ours are beyond the ken of our medieval ancestors, to whom the idea of progress would have been simple blasphemy.

Part Three

Related Ideals

XIII.

Freedom and Justice

THE MOST persistent and troublesome source of confusion in thought about freedom is the equation of freedom with other cherished goods. It is troublesome, however, because it is not simply arbitrary or perverse. It springs from deep, close connections with other ideals. Thereby it sets a nice problem: the need of clearly distinguishing them, but without divorcing them. And this is no mere verbal problem for logicians to settle, for when freedom emerges historically as a conscious ideal it is always entangled with other ideals that have much to do with its form and pressure, its risks and costs.

A primary example is the indispensable, universal idea of justice. Freedom and justice have been wedded so long in common usage that they are often said to be one and inseparable. In the free world justice means first of all equity, an even-handed judgment in accordance with a law that is no respecter of persons. Its cardinal principle is equal rights to life, liberty, and the pursuit of happiness. Tyranny, serfdom, slavery are *ipso facto* unjust; so it follows that the long struggle for freedom has been a struggle for justice. Yet the very assertion that they are one and inseparable intimates that these terms are not actually synonymous. The word *justice* does not appear in the common dictionary definitions of freedom, nor *freedom* in the definitions of justice. From the long struggle for freedom it also follows that these ideas have been historically separable. It took many centuries to abolish slavery because this was all the while a legal institution, defended as just by eminent philosophers and churchmen, endorsed by God himself in the Old Testament. Plato and Aristotle stated the logic of almost all law codes in antiquity when they argued that justice does not consist in giving equal rights to men who are naturally unequal—it consists in giving every man his due; or in other words, the law *should* be a respecter of persons. On the record, justice is a much older idea than freedom, considerably broader, at once more universal and more variable.

All societies have had laws, written or unwritten, to which most of their members conformed with little or no question or complaint. The accepted codes naturally embodied many diverse ideas of what is right or just. In most civilized societies they conferred power and privilege upon the few, drastically restricting the freedom of the many. They not only legalized oppression but made it harsher by what seem to us cruel punishments; they were more despotic because law was commonly regarded as God-given, not man-made. When the early civilizations attained to conscious ideals of social justice, proclaimed in royal codes or religious scriptures, these ideals fell far short of the bills of rights and civil liberties we cherish. The primary object of law was to maintain the *status quo,* not to secure liberty, much less to expand it. When the word *free* began to appear in the codes, it was chiefly to distinguish the status of the unfree—the slaves. In Hittite law, for example, a slave was worth exactly one half a free man for purposes of compensation or restitution for injury.

Gains in personal freedom, on the other hand, do not automatically assure more social justice. They may entail new modes of oppression, as the poor learned when laissez-faire individualism was made sacrosanct by Supreme Court decisions; freedom became a right to exploit other men. One distinctive sign of a free society, indeed, is a constant tension between the ideals of freedom and justice, reflected in every political debate. Moreover, hardheaded thinkers have long been questioning the legitimacy of their historic marriage. Historicists point out that ideas of justice are historically conditioned, mere matters of custom. Legal positivists assert that it is logically impossible to declare any law unjust, because it is law that determines justice. It would appear that tyranny is only a convention, and that freedom must shift for itself.

One may suspect, however, that hardheaded Anglo-Americans have cut justice loose because they take for granted democratic rights and principles of justice. In Hitler's Germany positivists might have found it possible to declare some laws unjust. Historicists might have objected to Hitler's substitution of "the feelings of the people" for the rule of law, especially when people felt like exterminating Jews. Few men who believe in civil liberties really believe that they are no more than expedient conventions. The constant tension between the ideals of freedom and justice springs from an actual connection between them, logically and historically.

To begin with, there can be no effective freedom in society without some principle of justice, rights assured by custom or law. If ancient codes most conspicuously imposed constraints, they also protected the individual against uncustomary constraints and gave him some rights; within his allotted sphere he was free to carry out his purposes. No code, to my knowledge, has declared the right of a ruling class to act on whim, to maim or kill the poor whenever the mood came over them. None has said in so many words that might always makes right. Historically, conscious ideals of justice have in the long run clearly tended to promote freedom for the many. The royal codes and religious scriptures of antiquity typically proclaimed a concern for protecting the poor against the rich and powerful, and if they as typically proved more or less ineffectual, they kept alive the idea of the rights of the poor, the need of safeguards against the abuse of power. In Israel the great prophets were indignant over the oppression of the poor; their impassioned denunciation of social injustice has kept ringing through Western tradition. And another basic principle in this tradition, to repeat, is freedom under law. The first liberty claimed by Englishmen was a demand for law, the right to be treated always under law—a principle of equal justice. We may agree with Thoreau that the law alone will never make men free, but we must add that they cannot be free without it.

The growth of freedom has in turn as clearly tended to promote the ideal of equity. If it has led to more strife among individuals, with new forms of injustice, it has led as well to a keener sense of injustice, a revulsion against inequities that under authoritarian regimes were routine. The extension of rights logically imposes a duty to respect the rights of others. Men may be inclined to neglect this duty, but the others have some means of asserting their rights, and all may be schooled in habits of mutual respect and fair play. The historical fact remains that the rights to life, liberty, and the pursuit of happiness came to be considered a basic principle of justice. Free men denounced the venerable institution of slavery as unjust. The grounds of such judgments, the issue of what constitutes "true" justice, will concern us later. Meanwhile it seems fair to conclude that in the democracies a love of freedom has generally gone hand in hand with a love of justice, and that neither ideal is secure without a love of both.

XIV.

Liberty, Equality, Fraternity

THE PRINCIPLE of equality that kept cropping up in the discussion of justice raises similar issues, but more difficult ones. The relations of liberty and equality, and of both with fraternity, once seemed clear and simple. They were united in a democratic trinity, fathered by a God who had created all men free and equal. Americans in particular have been pleased to recite that their nation, conceived in liberty, was dedicated to the proposition of equality. Yet most of their Founding Fathers were not actually dedicated to this proposition. Many avowed champions of freedom, such as De Tocqueville and Lord Acton, have held that these ideals are not only distinct but basically incompatible: the more equality men enjoy, the less freedom, or the more freedom, the less equality. Today some thinkers are asserting that the principle of equality is the very source of modern despotism, or in other words that it is an enemy of both freedom and justice.[1] In

---

[1] One instance is *Liberty or Equality*, The Challenge of Our Times, by Erik von Kuehnelt-Leddihn. As a Catholic monarchist, he is no friend of democracy, but he is cited respectfully by the "new conservatives" in America.

some intellectual circles this idea has become almost as popular as Original Sin.

Now the principles of freedom and equality are clearly not identical. By any common definition of freedom, it does not logically follow that all men are equally capable of it or deserving of it. As men go about choosing and carrying out their purposes, nothing is more obvious than the natural inequalities in intelligence and ability, the basis for claims to special privilege. In history, accordingly, the principles have not come down hand in hand. Ancient Greece led the way toward freedom with no universal ideal of equality, its citizenry frequently being outnumbered by their slaves. For centuries Christian churchmen preached spiritual equality and the brotherhood of man while remaining indifferent or hostile to political freedom. The English have long been jealous of their liberties, but until recently they had no strong sentiment of equality, maintaining with pride a privileged aristocracy. The authors of the American Constitution virtually repudiated the proposition stated in the Declaration of Independence; a major reason for the elaborate system of checks and balances they devised was to protect men of property against the popular will. Only well along in the last century did suffrage become universal. Only in this century has the principle of equality been applied to women, who all along made up half of the human race.

Similarly these principles may conflict. Freedom may menace the ideal of equality, as it conspicuously did under the gospel of *laissez faire*. Increasing inequality in wealth and power was then justified by the competitive principle of the survival of the fittest—scarcely a fraternal principle. No less plainly, equality may menace freedom. As De Tocqueville feared, it may lead to the tyranny of the majority, or of public opinion. It has inspired such elementary fallacies as William Jennings Bryan's argument in defending the ban on the teaching of evolution, that equality before God means that "all men are equally good biologists before the ballot box of Tennessee." It can take uglier forms, such as McCarthyism. But most persistent, pervasive, and insidious are the social pressures to conformity and uniformity, the unlegislated constraints on independent thought and unconventional behavior—a "slavery without masters." In America, where the sentiment of equality has been most pronounced, so has the fear of being different, the suspicion of men who dare to be different. In no other country could a man be sued because he painted his mailbox white with black lettering instead of black with white lettering, like all the others in the housing development.

The proposition that every man ought to be respected and so far as possible allowed to be his own master, make his own choices, pursue happiness in his own way, has never been easy to square with the facts of life; but it has become harder to do so in a materialistic mass society. The public opinion that sets the means and ends of self-realization is the opinion of the ordinary man on the street. Usually he is pleased with his ideas and tastes, which for the most part are not really his own. He confuses the right to one's own opinion with the idea that any opinion is as good as any other. The one exception he makes is with uncommon opinions, of radicals or eggheads. He has little passion for the maintenance of freedom of thought and speech, the liberal principles that have established his own rights. He resents cultural authority, the effort to maintain standards of excellence. For him everything must be made easy, or his money back. And now mass industries are geared to the exploitation of his tastes and the manufacture of his opinions—the business of telling him who he is, how he feels, what he wants, in a brave new world of private unenterprise and irresponsibility.

Once more, however, there remain sound reasons for the traditional association of the ideals of freedom and equality. Only on the grounds of a principle of equality can serfdom and slavery be condemned as unjust; only with some assurance of equal rights can all men hope to enjoy effective freedom. Democracy is now in fact wedded to this principle. The reasons become clearer when we consider the logical and historical alternative, a society based on the assumption of natural inequality.

In theory an aristocracy might grant civil liberties to the many, and take pains to safeguard their rights. In practice it naturally denies them political freedom, a voice in their government or in the determination of their rights, and as naturally it tends to restrict their social opportunities. All through history exclusive rule by the few has meant the subjection of the many, when not harsh oppression. Thus medieval thinkers had some lofty things to say about Christian liberty, but medieval society was far from being a free society because it was on principle a hierarchy, with a mass of serfs at the bottom.

From the beginning, therefore, the struggle for freedom in the Western world has been predominantly a struggle for more equality, against the hereditary privileges of the few. It came to a head in the French Revolution, which put an end to feudal privilege. Thereafter the leaders in the struggles against slavery, and for the rights of workers and of women, perforce appealed to the principle of equality. (The Bible, to which they initially appealed, provided more texts for the opposition.) By now most men in the democracies have come to agree that positive freedom requires not only equal suffrage and equality before the law but some measure of equality of opportunity, through free public education.

As with justice, there also remains a constant tension between the ideals of freedom and equality. A champion of freedom may consider it the primary ideal, as a safeguard against the dangers and abuses of egalitarianism; or a champion of equality may claim as much for it as a safeguard against the dangers and abuses of freedom. Their relations in the democracies are in any case so close that analysts are unable to agree on which is the stronger force or the greater danger. (Followers of De Tocqueville, including the "new conservatives," see equality as the ruling passion of Americans, and worry chiefly over the tyranny of the majority; Herbert Schneider and others assume that in their competitiveness Americans are disposed to sacrifice equality to liberty.) But as everybody is for freedom and justice in theory, while many attack the ideal of equality on principle, we might look at this ideal more closely. Its enemies are also liable to some elementary fallacies.

No sane democrat denies the actual inequalities of men. The author of the Declaration of Independence was not such a simpleton as to believe that men were literally created equal; the need for equal rights derives from their very inequalities in ability, which enable some men to dominate others. Neither does the ideal necessarily call for an absolute equality in social condition, the dream of utopian Communists and the nightmare of Christian businessmen. Its supporters have always disagreed over the extent and the kinds of equality they think feasible or desirable. They have agreed primarily on a principle of moral equality, that men should be treated as if equal by virtue of their common humanity, and ideally should all be given a fair chance to realize their best selves. This principle is implicit in all the higher religions, if neglected in practice by most of the established churches: the great religious teachers have offered a good available to all men alike. And despite the wide differences among men, the principle of equality has a plain natural basis in the fact of their common humanity—their common possession of mind, their common needs and desires, their common pursuit of happiness, and above all their common fate of death. In the face of death all differences may be forgotten. As Chesterton noted, the cry that goes up is "*Man* overboard."

One may still maintain that it is better, especially in the interests of high culture, to aim at the fullest possible freedom for the gifted few rather than for the ordinary many. Today conservatives are fond of citing Irving Babbitt: "One should in the interests of democracy itself seek to substitute the doctrine of the right man for the doctrine of the rights of man." But such aristocratic thinkers almost invariably dodge the obvious questions. Who decides who is the "right man"? How do we go about getting and keeping him in the right place? Can we, without the safeguard of rights, trust him to do the right thing? In our technological society the natural aristocrat is presumably the expert; but even if we could agree on a method of selecting and installing experts, and delegating authority to them, we could be sure only that they would disagree among themselves, that the majority of them might be wrong, and that ordinary people would bear the brunt of their mistakes. Experts themselves illustrate another significant element of equality in men—their common fallibility. They point to another argument for both freedom and equality, that men cannot agree on the means and ends of the public welfare.

Since it is now fashionable to worry over the tyranny of the majority, and to ridicule the basic irrationality of equal suffrage for morons and experts, it is well to keep an eye on the historical alternative and its basic irrationality. Throughout history the most conspicuous tyranny has been the tyranny of minorities; privileged classes have never given the many a real chance to realize their best selves. Nor have they themselves had a clear, rational right to their privileges. While openly or tacitly claiming a natural superiority, aristocracies have always depended on coercion to maintain their superiority, have never been willing to let nature take its course; and so they have repeatedly succumbed to the selfishness, greed, and stupidity they feared in the masses. Furthermore, men have never been able to agree on a uniform standard of superiority. It might be valor, intelligence, learning, virtue, holiness, social grace, artistic ability, military prowess, administrative skill, or even shrewdness in money-making. But by any standard members of ruling classes have fallen short, and at their best they have never been clearly superior on every count.

The simple truth is that men are neither equal nor unequal in all respects. The "common man," who is by definition mediocre, is not mediocre in every respect. He may be a better husband, parent, friend, craftsman, soldier—even a better citizen—than his critics. We must still generalize about his tendencies and his capacities, given a mass society with equal suffrage. But we must also keep aware that we are generalizing or abstracting, that the crude labels of "mass-man" and "elite" conceal the countless kinds and degrees of interest and ability, and that the faults of America run from top to bottom. Remembering that common men have been getting their first real chance in history, we might reconsider the historic record.

This at least belies the traditional belief from Plato on that equality means rule by the unruly mob, brings on the constant threat of disorder, civil war, anarchy, finally tyranny. These are real dangers, especially in the early stages of struggle against privilege; men with grievances, and without education or political experience, are unlikely to be sober and judicious. Yet civil war and anarchy are hardly serious threats in America, England, Scandinavia, and other established democracies.

The philosophical predisposition to regard hierarchy as the most natural and illustrious kind of order led thinkers to overlook the possibility that equality might be a means to a stabler political order. In America today the most apparent danger is not disorder but too much order, of a hierarchical kind. The political tyranny of the majority is still less conspicuous than the power of organized minorities or pressure groups. And the aristocratic thinkers who are attributing modern despotism to the principle of equality are simply ignoring the plainest historical facts. Such despotism grew up in Germany, Czarist Russia, Catholic Italy and Spain—countries with a strong aristocratic tradition, and no political tradition of liberty and equality; Mussolini, Hitler, and Stalin alike explicitly rejected the principle of equality. So far the despotism has been most vigorously opposed by the established democracies.

More serious, on the face of the record to date, have been the cultural costs of the principle of equality, the social pressures against individuality in an increasingly standardized society. These, however, have been due not merely to the power of the "common man," but to the forces of industrialism and commercialism. And they may seem less grievous if we consider the related ideal of fraternity, to which almost everyone pays at least lip service. The relation is again not simple or one-to-one: brothers are not necessarily free and equal, nor are free men necessarily brotherly. But again these ideals are in fact related. A lord and his serfs may maintain decent human relations, even get along better than free men or actual brothers. Only free men who regard themselves as substantially equals can feel and act like brothers. They may then work better together, with more energy, enterprise, and enthusiasm. Another consequence of the ideal of equality has been its practical utility in promoting co-operation, on the basis of self-respect. The conformism and complacence it has induced may seem worse because we take for granted the spirit of personal independence it first induced. We assume that men naturally should not be so servile as most were in the past. We forget the world of difference between the American man on the street and the historic peasant.

XV.

Natural Law and Natural Rights

IN BEGINNING with an appeal to "the laws of Nature and Nature's God," the Declaration of Independence was harking back to an idea that had come down from Greek philosophy through Cicero. "True law," Cicero declared, "is right reason in agreement with nature." Since by nature all men possess reason, he went on to define it as a universal law, "unchanging and everlasting": a principle of justice applying equally to all men and above all actual laws, which reflect "bad habits and false beliefs." In passing into Western tradition, this concept of "natural law" took on the authority of God. Implicit in it was a constitutional principle, a limit on the power of monarchs, who were under this higher law. Ultimately "right reason" derived from it the doctrine of natural rights. "Human rights," wrote Voltaire, "should be founded in all cases on the law of nature." On this basis the Declaration of Independence proclaimed the "self-evident" truth that all men are endowed with inalienable rights to life, liberty, and the pursuit of happiness.

Here, then, is the historic charter of our liberties; and not one of its articles is actually a self-evident truth. It is a string of what may now be called glittering generalities. "Right reason" comes down to my reason, which is never the same as the other fellow's. No such natural law is universally recognized, no human law is "unchanging and everlasting." "Nature" remains ambiguous, but in its most common meaning of the physical universe it authorizes no law of justice, endows men with no more rights than any other animal; its plainest law is the law of the jungle. In human affairs "natural" can mean almost anything, from the customary to the ideal—to the opposite of the actual or seemingly most natural. The rights proclaimed in the Declaration of Independence are so far from being natural in this latter sense that the great majority of men in the past never enjoyed them. Grant the principle and men still cannot agree on just what rights are natural. None is in fact inalienable, not even the right to life. The freest societies require men to give up their lives in time of war.

But let us forget "Nature" for a moment and translate the glittering generalities into a question. *Ought* all men to have the rights to life, liberty, and the pursuit of happiness—so far as possible, so long as they obey the law? Now most of us would answer yes. If positivists tell us that no statement containing an ethical *ought* is logically demonstrable or purely meaningful, let us consider this statement: children ought not to be beaten to death. Who would disagree? Like tyranny and slavery, torture has been common enough to be called "natural," yet we consider it unnatural too. We do not really believe, once more, that all these practices are merely matters of custom or convention, or merely poor policy. We believe that they are simply *wrong*. While we may condone them in the past as products of "the times," we still believe that they are always wrong. And if so we are committed, it seems to me, to something like the traditional doctrine of natural law and natural rights. As we value freedom, we at least cannot afford to dismiss them out of hand as only glittering generalities.

For the same reason we cannot afford either to ignore the plain objections to them. Law is man-made, not written in the constitution of nature, and it unquestionably embodies the different customs and beliefs of different societies. Cicero himself gave away the element of convention when he cited an example of natural law: "No one shall have gods to himself, either new gods or alien gods, unless recognized by the State." The convention is no less apparent when nature's God is made the author of law. Christians have rejected some of the laws that God supposedly wrote into the Bible (though it took them a long time to drop the command "Thou shalt not suffer a witch to live"), while they continue to disagree about the divine will in other matters, such as divorce. Belief in a divinely ordained law has generally been hostile to the cause of freedom, indeed, as it sanctified the temporal customs of unfree societies, and God has everywhere been much more explicit about the duties than about the rights of men. Likewise the principle of an immutable law is a natural boon to conservatives. In the last century every major social reform, from compulsory education to factory legislation, was opposed as contrary to natural law or God-given rights. Hence liberals in this century attacked the doctrine of natural law on pragmatic grounds, so that law might be more freely adapted to changing conditions and needs.

Nevertheless law cannot be changed or adapted without some standard of judgment, some end in view. These liberals were judging by democratic standards, seeking more justice for common men, and they were inclined to appeal to "simple humanity." Granted that law always embodies chiefly convention, the issue remains whether it represents *mere* convention and any judgment of it is *mere* opinion. My belief is that short of an everlasting, immutable law authorized by God or nature, we can find something like universal principles of justice, grounded in the nature of man and society, which support the principle of natural rights and therefore the ideal of freedom.

To begin with, law itself is a universal of human culture, like morality. It is everywhere respected and obeyed, at the expense of the individual's sweet pleasure. The widespread belief that it was divinely ordained reflected the common belief that it was not merely a matter of expediency or utility. As Cicero argued, if utility is the only standard, there is no good reason why men should not break the law whenever they find it possible and profitable to do so; yet lawbreakers have generally been the exception. And beneath all the diverse codes and conventions we can make out some common principles of justice, based on the absolute needs of man as a social animal. As he has to be able to count on the behavior of his fellows, all codes require him to keep his plighted word, at least to members of his own group. All prohibit theft, rape, and murder. With the growth of civilization, the principles underlying such general agreements became clearer and more conscious, most obviously in the wide area of agreement on ethical principles in the higher religions. With the rise of great nations came efforts at international law, an approach to the formulation of universal principles. At least in theory, to repeat, men are generally agreed that might does not make right. Such agreements on principle have now become an absolute need for the survival of civilization.

Thinkers who assert that all ideas are historically conditioned may therefore still "explain" these developments; yet they imply that this idea of theirs is not so conditioned. They offer it as a valid insight, an objective truth—and presumably it might help us to make better judgments. They may overlook, too, the positive knowledge that conditions our judgments. We can understand the pathetic fears that once wrote laws against witches, but we may be confident that historicists and legal positivists would oppose a revival of these laws. Similarly the vagueness of "right reason" may obscure the elementary necessity of an appeal to reason, and the positive element of rationality in all civilized codes of law. We would all agree, for example, in condemning as unjust a law that sentenced all red-headed men to the loss of their right arm, all bald men to death. If asked why we agree, we would begin by saying that such a law is wholly arbitrary, patently unreasonable. We might then become aware of a principle of impartiality or equal justice implicit in law by its nature, as binding on all members of a society. Although in ancient law this principle was obscured by special privilege, it at least applied to all holders of a given status; and so it might logically be extended, as in time it was, to the whole community, because it is implicit in the nature of community too. Equal justice might then be called a "natural law."

We might also say that a law against redheads and baldheads would be a violation of elementary human rights—you can't do such things to people without cause. We would then be verging on the principle of "natural rights." But here again we need first to review the plain objections to the traditional doctrine of rights as God-given, or enjoyed in "a state of nature," or founded on "a law of nature."

Whatever God's plan may be, man has got from his society whatever rights he has enjoyed, and is endowed with them at birth only in the sense that the infant at once becomes a member of society. The rights that seem natural to Americans are historically rare, and were won against the opposition of God's most authoritative spokesmen. The inevitable disagreement over just what rights are natural was intensified by confusion over their source. Thus the property rights that Locke helped to make primary were most clearly due to society or the state, not to God or nature; but private property acquired sanctity, the more readily as businessmen found that the way to help God was to help themselves to a lot. (Locke was conveniently silent about the many men who had no property.) The confusion became grotesque when literally soulless corporations laid claim to the inalienable rights of man, though to judge by Scripture, God himself never dreamed of anything like U.S. Steel.

All the same the principle of natural rights does have a natural basis, in the constitution of a social animal. Men in all societies have had some idea of rights, however cloudy or unconscious. It is inseparable from the universal acceptance of duties, which involve rights of other members of the community. Logically, one cannot deny men any rights and still demand their obedience, claim their allegiance, insist on their recognition of duties. Prior to logic remains the simple fact of our common humanity, the source of natural sympathy and fellow feeling. Out of this flowered the respect for the human spirit implicit in all the higher religions. And such respect carries us beyond logic, or specifically beyond the principle of social utility that Bentham and Mill tried to substitute for the abstract principle of natural rights. Bentham's standard of the greatest happiness of the greatest number implied that the pursuit of happiness was a kind of natural right. Mill's fervent argument for the social necessity of freedom and the social value of individuality more clearly sprang from a reverence for life, a felt conviction of the sanctity of personality. He would unquestionably have condemned Hitler's persecution of the Jews, even though it conceivably might have made most Germans happier, and as unquestionably he would have opposed the dictatorship of the Soviet, even though it has plainly made Russia a more vigorous, prosperous, materially progressive society. It is not mere utility that makes most of us believe in the absolute right of all men to have rights.

Just what rights will remain forever debatable. It is surely reasonable to begin with life, however, and not unreasonable to add liberty and the pursuit of happiness—so far as possible to give all men an opportunity to realize their humanity, and to enjoy the elementary goods that make life worthwhile. That most men in the past got along without such rights and opportunities is true but beside the point, for only those who have enjoyed them can realize how precious they are. The doctrine of natural rights proclaimed in the American and French Revolutions, and soon ridiculed by most political thinkers, nevertheless spread all over Europe and South America. In the guise of "human rights" it has now spread all over the world, as an accepted principle of the United Nations. Although many countries obviously deny human rights in practice, few do so openly, on avowed principle; coercion and tyranny have to masquerade as means of promoting the welfare of "the people." Still more remarkable is the wildfire spread of the idea of the rights of women—an idea that in one generation has won virtually universal acceptance, though it was foreign to both the religious and the political traditions of most peoples.

All this by no means proves the absolute or self-evident truth of the doctrine of natural rights. But its universal appeal does make evident the naturalness of rights, the possibility of general agreement in theory on universal principles of justice. And it suggests that man has potentially more desire for freedom than most of his history would intimate.

XVI.

The Nature of Democracy

ALTHOUGH in common discourse *democracy* means a free society, these terms too are not necessarily synonyms. Some ardent apostles of freedom, notably Voltaire, had no ardor for popular government. Jacob Burckhardt could say that he hated democracy because he loved liberty. As in theory "rule by the people," it embodies the principle of equality that may jeopardize freedom. As in practice rule by the majority, it may not secure the rights of minorities. It can foster a tyrannical worship of the state—*my* country, right or wrong—that not only threatens the freedom of other peoples but at home makes treason of dissent. America, a nation founded on the declared right of revolution, now requires its teachers to sign loyalty oaths, swear that they will never under any circumstances advocate revolution.

Nevertheless there is no real question that democracy has been a primary factor in the growth of freedom, both as cause and as effect. A distinctively Western institution, it is the most apparent reason why Western peoples have enjoyed more freedom than Eastern peoples. If monarchical or aristocratic government can be benevolent, enlightened, and responsible, all history makes clear that the rights and interests of the many are never secure unless the many have some voice in their government, some constitutional means of holding their rulers responsible. Their rights may not be secure under democracy either, of course; but it has indisputably made them freer, given them more opportunity for self-realization.

The real issue is the essential nature of democracy. It is scarcely a precise term, considering the various historical kinds and degrees of popular government. One might find it hard to say at just what point in its history England became a full-fledged democracy, since the "Glorious Revolution" of 1689 that secured the liberties of Englishmen left most of them without effective representation in Parliament. Today its meaning has been widely confused, both by champions of the Soviet who proclaim that Communism alone represents "true" democracy, and by champions of American democracy who identify it with national fetishes like federalism and capitalism. Such confusion, however, is mostly shallow or synthetic. It is still not too hard to make out certain common means and ends that follow logically from the basic idea of government of, by, and for the people.

In the established democracies men are generally agreed that government must include political means for enabling the ruled finally to control their rulers, and that among these means must be the vote, without intimidation. Sophisticates can easily ridicule popular notions of government by the people, or the annual spectacle of uninformed voters marching to the polls to express their confused will. Strictly, the people

never rule, always a few must rule, and often their policy may
not represent majority opinion, even if the majority happen to
have a clear, definite opinion. Still, all voters have a chance
to put in their say; the majority does speak the last word in
elections. The ruled can always change their government, and
periodically do so. Worship of the state is tempered by criticism of the government, which is invariably made up of men
whom many voters regard as rascals and hope to kick out in
the next election. Democracy has usually been most vigorous
under a two-party system, but in any case it logically requires
the equivalent of a party system, some provision for organized
opposition to the men in power.

This in turn requires the freedoms traditionally associated
with democracy—freedom of speech, freedom of the press,
freedom of association. The authors of the Bill of Rights neglected to include private economic enterprise, which businessmen came to regard as the most fundamental freedom, but
this oversight was pardonable. Most fundamental for democracy is freedom of mind—of thought and speech, in learning
and teaching. Assured the right of free inquiry and above all
free criticism, which was denied by most political and religious
systems in the past, men might decide on both the values and
the abuses of free private enterprise, and on the legitimacy of
the tariffs, franchises, subsidies, and other favors that private
enterprise has always sought from the government. For democracy is not merely government by consent of the governed
—men in past societies habitually consented to government

by king, emperor, or pharaoh. The essential thing is free, rational consent, in an awareness of alternatives.

The primary importance of these means to popular control of the rulers has been made clearer by the rise of one-party rule under the dictators. Leaders in the so-called "people's democracies" today may be popular, may be ruling in the best interests of the people, may be sincere in their professed goal of a classless society with freedom and equality for all. Meanwhile it is nonsense to say that their regimes are "truly" democratic or that their people enjoy political freedom. Voters offered a single slate by the single party, given no choice between rascals at the top, denied the right of free criticism and organized opposition, and threatened with punishment for deviant opinions, have no effective political control over their rulers. The rulers testify to the popularity of democratic institutions by their concern over maintaining the appearance of elections, but they have not yet risked giving their people the essential freedoms.

Although tyranny under a privileged hierarchy would seem to be an illogical way of preparing for a classless society, it seems worse because of the declared ends of democracy. These include the ends of all government, such as order and security, but historically and logically they have involved as well the distinctive ideal of justice conceived as equal rights, with a respect for the individual and for the claims of conscience. Freedom itself has been conceived as not merely a useful means but an end, a sacred right. While it may be argued that such principles are expedient or the best policy, they are essentially moral through and through. As free societies the democracies have been open societies, but they have not been open to any kind of political experiment; government has been required to respect these principles. Granted that the democracies have everywhere fallen short of their ideals, they have nevertheless written the ideals into their laws and constitutions. The preamble of the typical constitution is a statement of high moral purposes.

Many political scientists now shy away from definitions of democracy in terms of its ends because these are necessarily cloudy, couched in hurrah words, and liable to be called meaningless. They prefer to confine its essence to its more definite, demonstrable means. Yet its declared moral ends cannot be ignored, even in a strictly empirical study. However cloudy, they have not only made democracy a potent historical force but have distinctly modified its means. Thus it has not in fact been the simple majority rule that its critics invariably attack. Everywhere it has declared certain rights inviolable, beyond the power of majorities to take away; everywhere it has given the individual some measure of freedom against the state, even though this is the people's state. And, granted its invariable shortcomings, it is in this respect, too, positively different from contemporary Communism. One can hardly imagine any of the established democracies liquidating a million or so of their citizens, as the Kulaks were openly liquidated in the Soviet. While proclaiming the democratic goal of a classless society, the dictatorships of the proletariat not only have shown a callous indifference to the individual, but on principle have denied him rights against the state, just as they have denied workers the right to strike. They illustrate most plainly the danger of separating means from ends.

Here again the celebrants of free private enterprise have profoundly confused the issues of freedom. They still boast of its superior efficiency, still chant that it is this that has made America great. Actually, Communism has been efficient enough—it has made Russia a great power in a single generation. It now looks more efficient than the American system, as Russia keeps gaining steadily in production while America stumbles on through periodic recessions and chronic unemployment. Business leaders and their representatives in the administration are the first to insist that the richest nation on earth cannot afford to spend proportionately as much on education, science, or even weapons as the Russians can. The reason why the rest of us are not simply dazzled by the Russian achievement is its human costs. The major issue between democracy and Communism is a moral issue. It comes down to the ideal of freedom—freedom not as expedience, but as justice.

Ultimately, the success of democratic means depends upon the vitality of democratic ends—upon how deeply, even unconsciously, the proclaimed ideals are engrained in everyday thought, feeling, and behavior. In many countries democratic forms have failed to establish genuinely popular government, or to secure political freedom, because democratic attitudes are not so engrained. Apart from ambition and greed, their politicians may be simply unable to perceive the necessity as well as the possibility of a loyal opposition; while the common people either acquiesce in the suppression of rival parties or encourage it by the violence of their partisanship. In the established democracies, on the other hand, men tend to overrate the value of their particular institutions. Americans still look upon their constitutional system of checks and balances as the main bulwark of their freedoms, although the British have done just as well without such a system, and although in recent times its most conspicuous effect has been to promote irresponsible government, reduce statesmanship to the arts of in-fighting, horse-trading, and log-rolling. What has kept America democratic has been not so much its slovenly, illogical political processes as sentiments and habits of fair play that Americans take for granted. It goes without saying—as it does not in most Asian or Latin American countries—that there will always be free elections, preceded by wide-open debate, and that the defeated candidates will always accept the result of the elections, just as the victors will suppress any impulse to jail or silence the opposition.

For the same reasons it is necessary to keep an eye on democratic society as a whole. Great power is now exercised willy-nilly, not only by the military and the heads of federal agencies, but by the oligarchies controlling the giant corporations, the mass media, the big labor unions and farm bureaus; and while we depend on these centers of power to offset one another, we also have to depend on the integrity and responsibility of the few leaders at the top. We have no easy political means of preventing their public relations men from exercising their inalienable right of free speech to conceal, misrepresent, and delude. We have therefore to depend also on a sufficiently intelligent, informed public opinion to help keep them responsible; and here too we must look beyond government, consider the social forces that mold opinion. The saying goes that Americans were free men before they declared their independence and set up their democracy. Today many do not look like free men when at work, in office, or on assembly line, or even when at leisure, staring at TV, having their brains washed by advertisers. Producers take pains chiefly to find out their "reactions"; and *reacts* suggests the twitching of a decapitated frog's leg when stimulated by an electric needle, not the free response of a human being. The fault is not their political rulers—these are still rascals due to be kicked out in the next election. The constraints on freedom of mind are so difficult to deal with because they are social, not political constraints.

EPILOGUE:

The Prospects of Freedom

THIS book could not in any case end in prophecy or confident prescription. The prospects of freedom must be uncertain if, as I have argued, man is free to make his own history; and I take it that no one would now deny his power to make it for worse—to end the history of our civilization. But the most obvious reason for uncertainty arises from the revolutionary forces of science and technology, which have at once given us an unprecedented power and drastically limited our freedom of choice in futures. We are bound by the conditions of an industrial order. This side of catastrophe, there is no going back to the simple agricultural society that many people prefer, no getting out of the One World that many patriots find distasteful; it is inconceivable that men will deliberately give up the power they have acquired through the machine. And we cannot anticipate the state of the world in the next century because we cannot anticipate the still more fantastic knowledge and power that men may then have.[1] Meanwhile it is hard

[1] Synthetic food, for example, might take care of the tremendous increase in the world's population that now poses alarming problems. Biochemists may discover what makes the grass green—a question that for a businesslike Secretary of Defense exemplified the futility of pure

enough for thinkers to keep up with the revolutionary changes that have already occurred, and with the ever-increasing pace of change. In this challenge—the effort to understand and to cope with the literally extraordinary conditions of human freedom today—lies the point of a necessarily inconclusive epilogue.

Immediately, the most dynamic political force in the world today is, of course, Communism. It may look like merely a new form of the old despotism, more evil because it has a power over both the minds and the bodies of men that ancient despots could never hope to have. It also looks like the speediest, most effective way of developing and organizing modern technology, at least for backward countries starting from scratch. Having made Russia a world power in one generation, it bids fair to make another such power of China. In another generation the Chinese, whose national existence Americans prefer not to recognize, may number a billion. America, on the other hand, has become a world symbol of conservatism. While conserving rather halfheartedly the ideals of democracy, it has been more devoted to business as usual, and to high standards of aimless or irresponsible living. It is only beginning to realize that in Communism it faces a serious economic, political, and moral as well as military challenge. The administration of a "dynamic" conservative—one that might have seemed relatively enlightened and progressive a generation ago—may prove to be the most disastrous in the

---

science, but that happens to be a very practical question, a key to manufacturing energy from sunshine.

nation's history, by its failure on every front to meet the challenge. In the nation's Capitol, an earnest recital of moral platitudes still passes for an effort at serious thought, and the supreme task confronting the nation is held to be balancing its budget.

In the world of thought (from which the Capitol often seems to be effectively insulated) it is possible to detect a similar backwardness. Intellectuals continue to size up our extraordinary situation in traditional terms, derived from radically different conditions of life. They are likely to be most persuasive but also most facile when dealing with the first and last questions. For these are the "timeless" problems—in which the times may nevertheless make a considerable difference. I am therefore returning to the basic issue I brought up at the outset: the nature of man.

The most familiar generalization about it has lately grown popular. You can't change human nature, goes the proverbial refrain—human nature is always the same. The many who have taken up this refrain always mean that man is naturally pretty bad, and they always speak in the name of realism, no less when they appeal to the mythical idea of Original Sin. Thus Clinton Rossiter states the premise of the "new" conservatism: "Man's nature is essentially immutable, and the immutable strain is one of deep-seated wickedness." Herbert Butterfield, speaking out of Christian tradition, condemns faith in human nature more roundly as a "disastrous heresy." And the upshot is perhaps more withering than they intend. "We must search for the source of our discontents in defective hu-

man nature rather than in a defective social order," Rossiter
concludes; but as this nature is immutably wicked, it follows
that we can really do little if anything about our problems.
Worse, there would seem to be little hope for democracy. If
man is as incorrigibly depraved as he is reputed to be, he is
simply not fit for freedom. The temporal and spiritual leaders
of the past who emphasized his depravity quite logically opposed the disastrous heresies of religious, intellectual, and
political freedom.

The plainest truths are on their side. All about us are the
ancient evils and follies of selfishness and self-righteousness.
Certainly you can't change the basic animal needs of man,
eradicate his proclivities to fear and rage, nor can you hope to
make an angel of him this side of the grave; it is safe to assume that he will always be prone to unoriginal kinds of sin.
Add that he is more a creature of custom or habit than of
primal instincts, and this is still far from saying that he is immediately or infinitely perfectible. Engrained habits are very
hard to change; no instinct seems more inveterate than his
disposition to resent and resist change in fundamentals. If the
diversity of his culture implies an essential plasticity, he is
never plastic enough for ardent reformers. And anthropologists have thoroughly discredited the romantic notion of a
naturally good creature who in the course of developing civilization somehow developed unnatural institutions that cor-
rupted him.

Yet his history suggests that the conventional idea of an
immutable human nature is shallow, provincial, strictly un-

realistic. In the long view man has changed so much that we can only conjecture about the nature of the prehistoric cavemen. We must often wonder, too, about the nature of the long-suffering masses in most civilizations. They hardly look selfish or wicked in their typically passive endurance; their "depravity" seems more a matter of ignorance and inertia than of the old Adam in them. About primitive men we may wonder just because we have come to know them much better, for they often defy current assumptions about human nature, often seem unaware even of an "acquisitive instinct." The ruling motive of economic self-interest in our own society, to which much of the evil of our times may be ascribed, is not "just human nature." Most societies have not sanctified the profit motive, but have subordinated economic activity to non-economic ends. Great revolutionary movements, from Christianity to Communism, have generally got under way by demanding self-sacrifice, not by appealing to economic self-interest.

Granted that man is frail and fallible, as any sensible man knows, the doctrine of Original Sin does not help much in understanding him, any more than it apparently has in getting Christians to behave themselves—they behaved scandalously in the pious Middle Ages. The doctrine is itself a product of a particular cultural tradition, and it illustrates the power of clichés in thought corresponding to the power of custom in behavior. To understand other traditions, and our own problems in a revolutionary world, we need to pay closer attention to the realities of cultural diversity and historical change. To understand our own Western tradition, we must realize that men refused to attribute their discontents to "defective human nature." They traced them to a defective social order, and they then set about to make over that order, develop democratic institutions. In so doing they made over themselves as well. One who believes in democracy must believe that social institutions, beginning with free public schools, make a real difference in behavior; but he has good historical reason for his belief. The nature of free Americans has been rather different from the nature of illiterate peasants.

In this view we might assess more realistically the significant change that seems to be coming over the nature of Americans —the growing conformism and "togetherness," the rise of the "other-directed" type and the "organization man." Probably the change has been exaggerated. At least De Tocqueville emphasized the conformity of Americans more than a century ago, declaring that he knew of no other country in which there was "so little independence of mind and real freedom of discussion"; and American writers from Cooper and Emerson on have continually made the same complaints. The conformity is not mere slavery either. It is a means to solidarity, and should warn us against the simple antitheses, as of individualism and collectivism, which are by-products of the radical dualisms of our tradition. The natural sociality of man may appear as intelligent co-operation or as slavishness, a high loyalty or a base conformity; just as his individualism may appear as self-respect or selfishness, the virtue or the evil of disloyalty. The Primal Curse, E. M. Forster noted, is not the knowledge of good and evil, but the knowledge of good-in-evil. At any rate, the conformism has little to do with Original Sin. It has much more to do with democratic institutions, the sentiment of equality, the traditional genius of Americans for associations. Today it has still more to do with the growth of huge organizations, alike in government, business, labor, and the world of entertainment.

It accordingly raises a rather different question about the prospects of the sons of Adam. The immediate menace to freedom is totalitarianism. In the long run the chief menace may well be the regimentation and standardization that are implicit in the very nature of a mechanized industrial society, and that have been on the rise in democratic as well as Communistic countries. A mass society is a massive threat at once to individuality and to genuine community, or to free personal relations. If we manage to avoid catastrophe, we might end in something like Aldous Huxley's Brave New World: a society of robots, all happy and hollow, perfectly conditioned and adjusted—the very ideal of some psychologists and specialists in "human engineering." In *Post-Historic Man,* Roderick Seidenberg argues that this will be the inevitable outcome of man's history. Viewing his whole history as a struggle between instinct and intelligence, in which intelligence is now gaining the upper hand, he foresees its eventual triumph, and with it a purely rational society, directed toward "fixity and permanence," in which there would be no room for individuality and spontaneity, and consciousness itself will finally disappear.

Man will at last achieve the social efficiency of the bees, ants, and termites. His budget will be permanently balanced.

We might like to say simply that "human nature" would prevent any such outrage—or in other words, the old Adam would save us. Nevertheless men can be conditioned, as the great majority in the past accepted a life of poverty and toil, and they conceivably might be conditioned to become still more like their machines, just as many technicians, copy-writers, editors, and public performers are already social neu-ters, willing to put their skills or their synthetic "personalities" at the service of any overlord who pays them. We must look further, I think, to ground our hopes for freedom.

One source of hope is the counter-tendencies implicit in the nature of an industrial society. Regimentation is not the only order of the day. Science and technology are still revolutionary forces, making for innovation and adventure, working against the stability that conservatives and dictators alike aspire to. The scientific spirit in particular remains a constant menace to conformity, a nuisance to all committees on un-American or un-Russian activities. Power in an industrialized society may be monopolized by a few, but the knowledge and the skills required to maintain such a society have to be widely diffused. Many more men have to be educated than in a sim-ple agricultural society; and men trained to think may keep on thinking for themselves. Even in the seemingly monolithic Communist order students are already giving trouble. Scien-tists have been permitted more of the freedom they require.

The growing realization that yes-men do not make ideal managers of industry may lead to more freedom of thought.

The apparent restiveness in the Communist world also suggests the most obvious source of hope—the whole Western tradition of freedom and individualism. This has made our civilization the most boldly, continuously, energetically creative civilization in all history, if by the same token it has made crisis almost its normal state. As L. L. Whyte remarked, never before has so much been owed to so many. Now we are at least not suffering the familiar fate of stagnation; there is still plenty of creative energy, there are still many given to experiment and adventure. And many who are unsubmissive, as unresigned. If by nature men have no passion for freedom, there remains the weighty evidence that they prize it once they have come to know it, or know of it. Communists may enslave workers and peasants, but they dare not call it slavery; they must call it "true freedom." In conformist America the tradition of individualism and dissent is live enough to have produced a growing awareness of the pressures against individuality, a growing protest. Even in their most slavish aspect as consumers—staring at TV, listening to commercials, buying chrome monsters with fins—other-directed Americans are evidently not wholly passive; for the men who sell them keep anxious, keep looking for new tricks. Everywhere subjected to incessant, high-powered pressures—in America to like and want what everybody else does, in the Communist world to obey and call their subjection freedom—common men still display some powers of resistance and rebellion.

There remain the powers of intelligence. Seidenberg notwithstanding, there is no immediate danger of too much intelligence—the wise money will bet on instinct for a long time to come. If thinkers are prone to ideals of "fixity and permanence," they are as prone to disagreement, and can be trusted to oppose the other fellow's ideal of fixity. In the free world most thoughtful men oppose all open efforts to regiment thought and behavior. The real issue is whether the powers of intelligence are strong enough, resilient enough, and widely enough diffused. Advertisers and publicity men, who ought to know the American public best, usually operate on the assumption that it is irrational, irresponsible, and immature; but their feverishness intimates the possibility that you can't fool all the people all the time. And now and then they gamble on the notion that many of the people have some capacity for adult thought and feeling.

In any case, all who believe in democracy are committed to this gamble. If we have any hope for a free society, we are obliged to assume its logical and moral responsibilities. We *must* risk the "disastrous heresy" of faith in human nature, even the nature of common men. Democracy grew up on this audacious heresy, and could not have grown without it. Defenders of the old order were always asserting that ordinary men are naturally selfish, greedy, fickle, and unruly, never to be trusted with freedom. "The Conservative's best of all possible worlds is already here," explains Rossiter; but it would not have been here except for the liberal faith in man, the liberal dream of a better world. It cannot be preserved by repudiating this faith, dwelling instead on "harsh doubts" about "the wisdom and possibilities of reform," while we perforce live in a revolutionary world in which we cannot sit tight. Now more than ever before men in the Western world need to reassert their unique faith, even to amplify their dreams of the future, set their sights higher; for in Communism they have to contend with a driving vision that has already won and made over much of the world. If they are done with dreaming, they are done for good.

Needless to repeat, our hopes for survival may very possibly be disappointed, and man prove unable to control the immense power he has acquired, the massive forces he has set in motion. The whole faith in a free society remains literally a faith. As I conceive it, it is a peculiarly difficult faith: one that implies fallibility and ultimate uncertainty by its very stress on tolerance and open-mindedness, that always invites risk or further uncertainty through the uses and abuses of freedom, and that can never offer the promises of miracle and mystery or the guarantees of authority. The maintenance of a free society, more than any other kind, requires arduous effort. But it may help to remember that if the ardors are necessary because of human frailty, they are worthwhile only because of human reasonableness, human decency, human dignity.

Date Due

OCT 2 4 1984

DEC